RSPB GUIDE TO BIRDWATCHING IN SNOWDONIA

D1783760

Written by ROGER LOVEGROVE

Illustrations by DARREN REES

Design and art work by JONATHON JENKINS,
Martine Blaney

Research by Rob Dean, Jane Mee, Mick Green

The RSPB wishes to acknowledge the help of the National
Trust, Nature Conservancy Council and Forestry
Commission for agreeing to the inclusion of several of their
sites in this guide. We also gratefully acknowledge the help
given by many individuals throughout Snowdonia who
have been generous in sharing their knowledge and have
thereby greatly assisted in this publication.

In particular we thank the Snowdonia National Park
Authority for encouraging this publication and
contributing substantially to its financing.

This publication was produced with the assistance of the
Manpower Services Commission.

ISBN No 0 903138 27 1

INTRODUCTION

This book has been produced by the RSPB as an introduction to birds and birdwatching in Snowdonia. The area is visited by well over two million people each year and most of these visitors take pleasure from the great beauty of the countryside and the richness of its wildlife. Some species of birds breed in Snowdonia each year and several occur as passage birds on migration or as winter visitors. The book outlines the status of the most regular of these birds and gives details of 49 of the best sites where the public is encouraged to go and see many of the species mentioned.

At the same time it is not claimed that the book is exhaustive. Plenty of other places in Snowdonia merit exploring for their birds and many may prove as rewarding as the sites included here. Deciduous woodlands, for example, abound in the valleys of Snowdonia — a good number have public footpaths through them and almost all support the characteristic birds which are featured in the sites included in this book. The same claim can be made for many moorland, riverside and coastal areas.

We do not pretend that the book is comprehensive in its coverage of all species which occur in Snowdonia. In particular the very commonest and most familiar — eg carrion crow, robin, house sparrow, blue tit — are as numerous here as elsewhere in Britain and are not therefore featured. Neither are those birds which are rare or accidental and consequently very unlikely to be seen by the general visitor.

Most of the birdwatching locations described in the book lie within the Snowdonia National Park but the boundary is not drawn rigidly and several sites around the periphery of the Park are included which are readily accessible to visitors and which are particularly good for birdwatching.

Note that the maps in the main section of the book are essentially diagrammatic and are designed to be of maximum use to the birdwatcher on site. For precise details of these areas it is essential to refer to the relevant Ordnance Survey sheets.

At all times birdwatchers are urged to observe the Birdwatchers' Code (see towards back). At a time when more and more people are regularly using the countryside, these considerations are more important than ever.

SNOWDONIA

Snowdonia is a land of spectacular beauty, rich in wildlife and infinite in its variety, moods and colours.

To appreciate this mountain land properly, its countryside, its people and its wildlife, requires above all else an appreciation of the antiquity of its origins and connections: to recognise that the form of the land, the origins of its people and the evolution of its wildlife lie deep down in the roots of time. On the northern foothills pre-Cambrian rocks — which extend over the Menai Straits and right across Anglesey — are the oldest known rocks on earth. The spectacular crags and deeply gouged valleys, chiselled from 'younger' (Cambrian and Ordovician) rocks, are the result of the endless action of ice, wind and water over 600 million years or more.

Snowdonia is the modern refuge and heartland of the Celtic race whose culture and language — far older than the hybrid English language which now contests it — flourish here with a fierce and proud tradition of politicians, poets and bards. Even the Welsh name for Snowdonia is so old that its origins are lost in the mists of time: Eryri 'the place of the eagles' (eryr is Welsh for eagle) . . . or does it derive more prosaically from the Roman 'oriri' — 'to arise' — ie the Highlands? In either event, this is the land more steeped in myth and legend than any other corner of our islands and rich in the visible relics of pre-history.

Fittingly, Snowdonia was one of the first National Parks to be designated in Britain in 1951. With this designation the interpretation of the name Snowdonia broadened almost overnight from the mountain core of Eryri to embrace a much wider area now including most of the old county of Meirionnydd south to the estuary of the River Dyfi. The National Park extends 50 miles from north to south and almost 35 miles from east to west, giving a total area of 845 square miles and making it the second largest park in Britain. Some two million visitors come to Snowdonia in the course of a year.

Fourteen of the peaks of Eryri are over 3,000 ft high. At 3,560 ft, Snowdon summit (Y Wyddfa) is the highest mountain south of the Scottish Highlands. The principal ranges in the Snowdon Massif are the Glyders, the Carneddau and the Snowdon group itself. Enormously deep valleys, eg Llanberis, Nant Ffrancon, Nantlle and Nant Gwynant, dissect these ranges and many of their precipitous walls are internationally renowned for rock climbing. The southern half of the Park includes the rugged spine of the Rhinog Mountains and the massive buttresses of Cader Idris and the Arenigs. Despite the large size of the Park and its proximity to the sea, there are only about 22 miles of coastline within its boundary. Almost all of this is on the coast of Meirionnydd in the west as the northern boundary of the Park falls just short of the north Wales coastline. Most of the Meirionnydd coast is low and sandy although there are a few miles of low cliffs running southwards from Fairbourne towards Tywyn.

Lying on the west side of the country and being as mountainous as it is, Snowdonia has a mild climate with a high rainfall. Snowdon summit is one of the wettest recorded places in Britain with over 120 inches of rain each year; 3,300 ft lower down, Beddgelert still has some 100 inches and Betws-y-Coed, in the shadow of the mountains, over 60 inches. Inconveniently for the visitor, summer is normally a fairly wet season and August is often particularly wet. Having said this, it is equally fair to add that there are many days which are bright, warm and sunny and even summer droughts are not unknown.

■ BIRDS IN SNOWDONIA

Snowdonia's birds are immensely varied. Their diversity reflects that of the countryside itself from the waterside, woodland and farmland birds of the Dyfi valley and coastal plain of Meirionnydd to the shore birds of the western estuaries and the upland birds of the wild mountains and moors of the Eryri.

Most of Snowdonia is rugged, powerful upland and in this mountain heartland four species perhaps symbolise Snowdonia. These are also four of the birds which visitors are keenest to see: two are members of the crow family and two are birds of prey.

The **raven** is extremely common throughout the Park and can be seen almost anywhere from coast to mountain top. It is so numerous that it often occurs in communal roosts and nesting pairs can be as close as one kilometre to each other in some areas. Nests are usually on vertical crags, but sometimes in tall trees, and favoured sites are used by generation after generation of ravens. The raven is a scavenger, relying heavily on plentiful carrion which is a by-product of the ubiquitous sheep industry in the hills. It is a large and powerful bird, half as big again as a crow and although pairs mate for life, birds not infrequently congregate in parties — sometimes up to a hundred strong — when surplus food is found. Its deep-throated, croaking 'prok prok', and frequent habit of rolling over in flight readily identify it from other members of the crow family.

The rarest of the British crows is the **chough.** It is a bird of cliff coasts, inland quarries and old mine shafts. Depicted on the cover of this book, it has shining black plumage and brilliant crimson legs and bill. Some 50 pairs occur in Snowdonia and some of the best places to see them are Bird Rock, Dinorwic Quarries and, in the winter, the Little Orme (maps 44, 14, 8).

Eagles have not nested in Snowdonia since the 17th century but the **buzzard** — so like a small eagle in its dark colouring, shape and soaring flight as to be quite easily confused by those not familiar with it — is very common. It breeds in virtually every Snowdonia valley where woodland or scattered trees occur in which the birds can nest. Buzzards frequently perch on telegraph poles or fences from which they search for small prey on the ground below. In flight they circle, glide and soar, seldom flapping their broad 'fingered' wings.

Most powerful and awe-inspiring of all the Welsh birds of prey is the **peregrine.** In winter it is frequent on the lower ground and along coasts but by March returns to the high crags to breed. Almost completely eliminated from Wales 25 years ago through the use of persistent agricultural pesticides, it has since made a dramatic recovery. Over 45 pairs now breed in Snowdonia — probably more than ever before. From March to July any high area of cliff is worth watching for peregrines. Dinas Mot, Dinorwic Quarries, Bird Rock (maps 15, 14, 44) are among the most reliable sites and the fortunate watcher may see the breathtaking speed with which the peregrine pursues other birds or makes the final stoop to kill.

raven

■ SUMMER WOODLAND BIRDS

Between late April and June the woodlands of Snowdonia are at their liveliest and most vital. Resident **tits, robins, nuthatches, woodpeckers, treecreepers, rooks** and **jackdaws** are joined by a host of migrant birds travelling north from Africa to a summer here in Britain. Under a fresh mantle of leaves and carpeted with anemone, wood sorrel, primroses and bluebells the woods now spring to life. As early as the end of March the first **chiffchaffs** arrive to join the rising volume of morning song from the resident birds. On woodland edges and open glades, **willow warblers** are the most numerous of all the summer visitors, and by early May a deluge of other warblers, flycatchers, redstarts and **tree pipits** has arrived. **Blackcap** and **garden warbler** are birds of the understorey in woodland and many of the Snowdonia woods, grazed hard by generations of sheep, no longer provide such a habitat and these two fine summer songsters are not as frequent as in many woodlands in England. Introduced rhododendron infests many woods in the National Park and although it is colourful and attractive when in flower it is spreading fast and is regarded as a severe pest. It has some benefits for birds such as blackcap and garden warbler however in providing a substitute shrub layer for them to occupy. The most characteristic warbler of the heavily grazed oakwood is the **wood warbler.** It is common throughout Snowdonia and is one of the most typical birds of these western sessile oakwoods. Its plaintive piping notes and shivering trill are a familiar woodland sound through May and June.

The male **redstart** is the most colourful of all our summer visitors and it abounds in these oak woodlands (and equally so in many open hillsides with scattered trees, derelict buildings or broken walls). By July many redstarts move out of the woods and can then be found along the narrow Snowdonia lanes often briefly flying ahead of your car before disappearing into a tall hedgerow showing a flash of a chestnut-red tail.

Perhaps the most popular and easily seen of the summer visitors to these old woodlands is the beautiful **pied flycatcher.** The males arrive first, usually in the third week of April and are followed by the females a week or so later. Like redstarts, they are hole-nesting birds and take very readily to nestboxes. The male's song is an abrupt but pleasing jingle and they are confiding birds which frequently give very good views. Once the young birds have left the nest in mid or late June, pied flycatchers abruptly 'disappear', resorting to the high canopy of the trees or moving out to overgrown hedgerows on the farmland.

Great spotted woodpeckers are common but the tiny **lesser spotted woodpecker** which is much less plentiful (and is more difficult to see) may also be looked for in alders or willows along riversides or lake edges. **Great tits, blue tits** and **long-tailed tits** are very numerous but both **marsh tit** and the very similar, but ecologically separate, **willow tit** are extremely scarce. Both species occur in the Conwy Valley (see maps 20, 13) but otherwise they are very difficult to find, especially the marsh tit. **Woodcocks** breed sparingly in these woodlands but are more frequent in winter when numbers are supplemented by continental immigrants. **Tawny owls** are numerous in most of the woods. Although they are crepuscular and nocturnal, they may sometimes be seen roosting in ivy-covered trees during the day time.

redstart

pied flycatcher

dipper

◼ RIVERSIDE, LAKE AND STREAM BIRDS

No bird is more characteristic of the fast boulder-strewn streams of Snowdonia than the **dipper.** This improbable bird is the only land bird which obtains all its food from the bed of these fast-flowing torrents. You can see dippers most easily from bridges — wait on the bridge and watch for 10 minutes and a dipper will almost certainly appear. Be still and quiet and you will see them walk or plunge under water and reappear a few seconds later.

Grey wagtails too are fond of the fast-flowing streams. They are summer birds, long-tailed, delicate and colourful. They feed on the flies and other small insects of the stream side and build a nest in the masonry of a bridge, wall or culvert. You may well encounter **goosanders** on the upper reaches of the larger rivers — Conwy (map 13), Mawddach (map 40) — for they are gradually increasing their numbers in North Wales. On the lower sections of the same rivers they are usually replaced by the commoner **red-breasted merganser** which is primarily an estuarine and in-shore bird. Both are fish-eaters — the goosander on small trout, eels and other coarse fish and mergansers on flat fish, gobies, ten-spined stickleback and elvers.

Kingfishers are not uncommon on these lower sections (particularly Afon Conwy) and **herons** too are more frequent by the slower waters although they may be found at almost any water-side from time to time, even in summer on the open moors where inexperienced young birds explore the boggy pools haphazardly for frogs and newts. **Sand martins** are uncommon in Snowdonia mainly because few of the rivers have suitable earth banks in which they can tunnel their nesting burrows.

Many of the Snowdonia lakes are poor for birds (see Wildfowl section) and the most frequent lakeside bird in summer is the **common sandpiper.** This long distance migrant lives by the stony margins of the lakes or shingle areas on the larger rivers and hides its nests in the grasses or thistle clumps nearby. Their teetering triple-note calls are a real summer sound of the upland waterside and like several other river birds (dipper, grey wagtail) they 'bob' incessantly as they stand on the water's edge.

◼ HILLSIDE BIRDS IN SUMMER

Bracken, and less frequently gorse, are the main vegetation cover of many of the steep, open hillsides in Snowdonia. Often these hillsides — 'the ffridd' in Welsh — are also scattered with hawthorn, rowan, holly or oak trees. In summer such places are rich in birds. Apart from the resident **yellow-hammers, chaffinches, stonechats** (commonest near the coast), **linnets** and **meadow pipits,** the ffridd is the summer home of several special visitors. **Whinchats** are often abundant — like stonechats they perch on prominent fronds of bracken or the twigs of hawthorn bushes from where the male delivers a pleasing jingle of notes. They can be extremely numerous on some of these warm, bracken-covered hillsides.

whinchat

Cuckoos are more numerous here than in any other habitat in Snowdonia and tree pipits, with their beautiful parachuting song flight, are especially attracted to these open hillsides wherever trees and bushes provide song posts. Redstarts are commonest where there is a loose scatter of trees on the hillside or when broken walls provide nest sites. Where short grazed turf exists and scree, rabbit burrows or broken walls provide holes for nesting, wheatears are to be found. They are common in many of the hill areas, conspicuous as they fly low across the ground displaying the clear white rump patch. The most abundant of the summer visitors is the willow warbler which thrives in great numbers on this ffriddland.

The warm hillsides are important hunting ground for kestrels, buzzards, sparrowhawks and sometimes merlins. In high summer many species of woodland and farmland birds bring their broods of young into the bracken areas where the protective cover is good and food is found in plenty.

■ BIRDS OF PREY

Wales is noteworthy for the numbers and variety of birds of prey. In Snowdonia eight species breed regularly. The most numerous is either the buzzard or possibly the sparrowhawk. Peregrines too are plentiful (see above). The kestrel — the most numerous bird of prey over much of Britain — is reasonably common in the Park, most likely to be seen either in the rocky valleys where quarries or low cliffs afford nest sites, or hovering over the many rough, bracken-covered hillsides.

The two moorland specialists, merlin and hen harrier, are now extremely scarce as breeding species in Snowdonia. They often nest in close proximity to each other and are principally found on

heather moorland, much of which has been lost since the last war to afforestation and agricultural improvement — now only one or two pairs of each still remain. In winter some of the coastal marshes, notably the Dyfi, are much better places to see them. Both can regularly be seen at Ynys-hir (map 49) as can short-eared owl and peregrine. It is strongly recommended that searches for hen harriers and merlins should not be made on moorland in summer — the observant casual watcher has as good a chance of seeing either bird on moorlands without causing disturbance. The same is true of the rare red kite, most beautiful of all European birds of prey, which just maintains a tenuous foothold in the Park.

female hen harrier

The goshawk (see also under Conifer birds) is increasing in numbers and may well be encountered in any of the large forests in Snowdonia. Like the sparrowhawk, it is most likely to be seen at a distance soaring or circling above mature woodland.

In early spring or late summer in most years several migrant ospreys are recorded in Snowdonia. Their appearance is unpredictable — they may be seen along rivers, estuaries, lakes or merely passing overhead. They usually move on the same day and none has yet made any attempt to nest in Wales.

buzzard

peregrine

■ COAST AND ESTUARY

The shores of Snowdonia have many stretches of low coast and fertile estuaries which are famous for the birds they support all the year round. These are rich feeding areas and among the best are Conwy estuary, Traeth Lafan and Aber Ogwen, Porthmadog Cob and Traeth Bach, Mawddach estuary, Broadwater, Dyfi. All these are included in the maps in the second section of this book and at most of them very good views of shore birds can be guaranteed.

Small numbers of **ringed plovers, redshanks** and **oystercatchers** still breed in some of these areas. At times of spring and autumn passage, and in winter, parties and flocks of other waders gather, sometimes in large numbers. **Dunlins** are usually the most numerous but **curlews, redshanks, oystercatchers** and **lapwings** are also common. Many other species occur especially at times of passage — **godwits, grey plovers, spotted redshanks, whimbrels, sanderlings, greenshanks** and **turnstones.**

Shelducks live on all these estuaries and also on low coastal areas such as Morfa Harlech and Morfa Dyffryn. They are large and conspicuous 'black and white' birds with red bill, bottle-green head and a chestnut chest band. **Red-breasted mergansers** are typical of these tidal estuaries, common on Traeth Lafan, Traeth Bach, Mawddach and Dyfi (maps 3, 27, 39, 49). Often in summer several broods will amalgamate to produce enormous 'families' or creches in the care of one or two females. **Eiders** are regular in most months off the Aber Dysynni.

Black-headed gulls and **herring gulls** (the latter being plentiful in all the seaside towns) are the commonest gulls. **Lesser black-backed gulls** occur on passage and as non-breeding summer visitors, but are otherwise not very common. In winter the **greater black-backed gull** is a frequent coastal scavenger, and **common gulls** are indeed common in most lowland coastal areas. **Cormorants** are ever present in all the estuaries, flying up and down the tidal reaches, swimming semi-submerged in the shallow waters or standing on sandbanks, boats or buoys, wings spread to dry in the wind. **Grey herons** stalk the shallows and creeks on the marsh edges and fly with bowed, laboured wings from one favoured feeding spot to another.

eider drakes

Skylarks, pipits, flocks of finches and buntings feed on the harvest of small insects and seeds from the grasses and other plants on the saltmarshes in autumn and winter. Also in winter peregrines, merlins and hen harriers hunt the marshes while ravens, carrion crows and jackdaws frequently scavenge on the shoreline.

On rocky shorelines look for the rock pipit, which is darker and a little larger than the meadow pipit and spends its entire life in the spray zone of the sea.

■ MOORLAND AND MOUNTAIN BIRDS

Snowdonia is most famous as a rugged land of mountains and wild, lonely moorlands. Some of its most notable birds are understandably those of these wild uplands. Early travellers relate many accounts of eagles in Eryri but these have long since gone. **Ravens, peregrines** and **buzzards** were other birds which always attracted attention and they still occur in high numbers and are great features of the Park. Sadly however much of the high, rolling moorland has changed dramatically in recent decades having been replaced by new conifer forests or emerald green sheep pastures. As a result of this, birds such as **red grouse, merlin** and **hen**

harrier are now very scarce on these Welsh hills. Small pockets of grouse occur where heather moorland remains but numbers are very small and it is a far cry from the days when moors such as Migneint (map 31) were justly famous for their bags of grouse each autumn. For much the same reasons hen harriers and merlins are now rare and moorland breeding waders — **golden plovers** and **dunlins** — are also scarce. **Curlews** and **lapwings** return to the uplands in late March and although they are no longer numerous anywhere throughout the Park, the Trawsfynydd area (map 30) and Hiraethog moors on the eastern boundary of the Park are among the best areas for both.

Meadow pipits and **skylarks** abound on the moorlands. **Ring ouzels** are not uncommon. It is a somewhat locally distributed bird however and is found most frequently in areas with broken cliff, heathery gullies, boulder clitters and sometimes in disused quarries; Rhinog (map 34), Arenig, Cader Idris and Aran are the favoured areas rather than the central massif of Eryri itself (but see Cwm Idwal, map 16).

The **short-eared owl** is a moorland bird but is extremely scarce throughout all Wales and very few pairs nest each year in Snowdonia.

male ring ouzel

■ CONIFER BIRDS

Large areas of Snowdonia are now covered with relatively new conifer woodlands, notably the extensive forests of Coed y Brenin, Gwydyr and Dyfi. For part of their growing cycle these forests are of extremely limited value to birds, mainly because they comprise mono-cultures of introduced tree species (eg Sitka spruce, Douglas fir).

In the first few years after establishment when they are fenced and sheep grazing is excluded, these young plantations do however support a wide variety of bird species and often have high populations of small mammals, especially field voles. Birds of prey then find them rewarding for hunting — **kestrels, merlins, buz-zards, short-eared owls, barn owls** and even **peregrines** or **hen harriers.** Breed-ing birds include species such as **willow warblers, whinchats, whitethroats, tree pipits,** and **grasshopper warblers** as well as commoner residents — **meadow pipits, wrens, robins,** and others.

Once the young trees are about 12 years old their canopies close together (thicket stage) and eliminate ground vegetation. The darkening forests then become particularly poor for birds. **Goldcrests, woodpigeons, chaffinches** (on the edges), **wrens** and **coal tits** are typical species at this time. The **goldcrest,** smallest of all our birds, occurs in most of these forests in spectacular numbers. Firecrests can occasionally be seen here too.

Today foresters are doing much to diversify these forests, and nowhere more so than in Snowdonia. Where the conifer forests are diversified, where different age groups occur close together and where there are wide clearings, open corridors along watercourses or a mix of deciduous trees, the forests become more interesting places for the birdwatcher. Several of the best forest birdwatching areas (maps 18, 21, 23, 35,

39, 48) are included in the later section of this book.

As the forests mature the **sparrowhawk** is the principal bird of prey, especially where larch occurs. It patrols the forest edge and the rides hunting for the smaller birds on which it preys. The larger and much rarer **goshawk** — closely related to the sparrowhawk — is increasing in numbers. It is a daunting bird, the female often as large as a buzzard, and is a fearsome predator which will take birds as large as black grouse! **Black grouse** do occur in Snowdonia as a forest edge species but they are now very scarce and it is a very lucky birdwatcher who sees one.

Two specialist cone-feeding finches are predictably increasing in numbers in these forests — **siskins** and **crossbills.** They are birds of the tree tops, most easily seen — especially if you know their calls — as they fly overhead. Look out on the ground for cones which crossbills have worked on. In winter large mixed finch flocks sometimes occur and involve a surprising number of species (see map 18). **Redpolls** are fairly numerous in these woods in spring although not restricted to conifer areas and are often found where birches are growing.

crossbill

siskin and redpoll

Where stands of older conifers are left to grow on they readily attract **buzzards** or **ravens** to nest in them. **Tawny owls** may occur there too and several of the other forest species, notably **siskins, crossbills** and **sparrowhawks** are even more likely to be frequent.

Many of the forest areas in Snowdonia are now being clearfelled and harvested before being replanted. These replanted ('restock') areas bring another spectrum of birds into the forest and as the young trees grow among the brash left after felling, several new bird species are attracted. **Tree pipits, blackcaps,** and **garden warblers** will use the area for several years as well as **whitethroats, willow warblers** and occasionally **yellowhammers** and **whinchats.**

■ BIRDS OFFSHORE

The shallow inshore waters of the Irish Sea are rich feeding grounds for seabirds. At times of spring and autumn passage many seabirds pass by just offshore and are easily visible from headlands such as the Great and Little Ormes, Mochras (Shell Island) and Aber Dysynni. **Kittiwakes, divers, gannets, fulmars, skuas** and **terns** can regularly be seen in late summer and autumn. **Little terns** formerly nested on most sand and shingle coasts but now only one tiny colony clings on in Snowdonia. **Roseate, common** and **arctic terns** are rather scarce passage birds (none breed) although at Traeth Lafan and Conwy Bay several hundred common terns are regular in August. **Sandwich terns** are the most frequent species offshore as a passage bird and non-breeding summer visitors from April to October.

Fulmars breed on the Great Orme and Little Orme and also on the low cliffs either side of the Mawddach estuary but elsewhere are not numerous. Promontories such as that at Aber Dysynni are good for sea passage of **Manx shearwaters** and **gannets.** During the breeding season the birds daily circle Cardigan Bay on their feeding routes. Off Dysynni there is almost always a non-breeding flock of **eider ducks** to be seen — the only ones regularly found in North Wales. This is also a good spot for seeing **divers** at sea, particularly **red-throated divers,** and sometimes **common scoters.** Scoters appear off Harlech fairly regularly in any month but the largest numbers are to be found off Llanfairfechan where several thousand can occur. They may also be seen off Conwy or the Orme headlands where **velvet scoters** and individual **surf scoters** have occurred each winter in recent years.

Off this northern coast in winter there are large numbers of **divers, red-breasted mergansers** and **grebes** especially at Traeth Lafan.

Guillemots and **razorbills** breed nowhere in Snowdonia except on the two Ormes and it is in the area of sea around here that they are easiest to see. The breeding colonies on the cliffs are very difficult to see from the land however. It is interesting to note that there are historical claims (c 1820) that guillemots bred regularly at Bird Rock, Tywyn, now land-locked and four miles inland, improbable though it may seem.

surf scoter

■ LOOKING FOR MIGRANTS

Coastal areas — particularly promontories or estuaries — are the very best areas to look for migrant birds in spring (March to May) and autumn (August to October). Around the coasts of Snowdonia several estuaries and headlands are notable places in this respect. Great Orme (map 7), and to a lesser extent Little Orme (map 8), are outstanding. Early **wheatears** appear here feeding on the short turf by late March, soon to be followed by **sand martins,** migrant **pipits, swallows, ring ouzels** and others — possibly **dotterels** or **yellow wagtails, cuckoos** or **hoopoe.**

In autumn, migrant **chats, buntings, thrushes** and **pipits** abound and are often joined by rarer species, perhaps a **shrike,** rare **warbler** or **bunting,** or passing **goldcrests, flycatchers** or resting **birds of prey.**

On the coasts of Cardigan Bay, Morfa Conwy (map 6) and Aber Dysynni (map 43) headlands are notable and both of these sites are equally good for in-shore migrants and off-shore passage of seabirds. From late July onwards the earliest of the northern waders will return again, firstly those which have failed to nest successfully and left their Arctic breeding grounds early. **Ruffs, green sandpipers, wood sandpipers** (freshwater pools) and **spotted redshanks** will be the first of these, often still in brilliant breeding plumage, and as summer stretches into autumn **curlew sandpipers, ringed plovers, godwits, turnstones** and **greenshanks** start to pass through. Many of the estuaries from Conwy to Dyfi attract these migrant waders. Among the best are Aber Ogwen and Traeth Lafan (map 3), Conwy (map 10), Traeth Bach (map 27), Porthmadog (map 25), Dysynni (map 43) and Dyfi (Ynys-hir, map 49). These rich and fertile estuaries also draw in other passing birds — various gulls and ducks, even rarities such as **egrets, ospreys** — and North American waders (October) or storm-driven **petrels** and **auks** may turn up.

wheatear

■ WILDFOWL

Mountain country is not the most suitable for wildfowl and indeed most species are poorly represented in Snowdonia. **Mallard** is the commonest duck and is found from sea level throughout the lowlands and foothills, even sometimes nesting on the moorland in bogs or peat hags up to 500 metres. In winter, flocks concentrate in a few lowland areas notably Traeth Lafan (map 3), Llyn Tegid (map 32), Traeth Bach (map 27) and the estuaries of Dyfi (map 49) and Conwy (map 10). **Teal** also congregate in the same areas but are otherwise thinly scattered inland in winter; a few pairs breed on coastal marshes and in upland bogs or around small vegetated pools in the hills. **Wigeon** are common in winter flocks in such places as Traeth Lafan, Conwy estuary, Porthmadog Cob, Traeth Bach, Mawddach estuary, Broadwater and Dyfi estuary. Other freshwater dabbling ducks, familiar in lowland Britain, **shoveler, garganey, gadwall, pintail,** are only scarce visitors. One or two favoured waters such as Trawsfynydd (map 30), Llyn Myngwl (map 45), Llyn Dinas, Llyn Nantlle, regularly attract small numbers of **tufted duck** between October and March (very occasionally pairs stay to breed.) **Pochard** too occur at this season and are regular in small parties on Llynau Gwynant, Padarn (map 14), Dinas Cwellyn, Trawsfynydd (map 30), Llyn y Gadair (map 17) and Llyn Myngwl (map 45).

Goldeneye are regular visitors to many estuarine and inland waters and **goosanders** are steadily increasing as breeding birds along some of the main Snowdonia rivers. (See also under Coast and Estuary, and Birds Offshore for other duck species.)

Mute swans are thinly scattered as breeding birds mainly on the lower land around the coasts and small winter groups of **whooper swans** are regular around Glaslyn Marshes, Morfa Harlech (map 33) and Llyn y Gadair (map 17), and occasionally on Llyn Cwellyn, Llyn Padarn (map 14) or Llyn Gwynant; often parties interchange from one site to the other. **Bewick's swans** are scarcer, most frequently seen briefly on inland or coastal waters as passage birds in autumn and early spring.

The most noteworthy — in fact the only regular — wild geese in Snowdonia are the **Greenland white-fronted geese** which winter on the Dyfi and reach a maximum of about 100. This is the only flock of this species to be found in England or Wales and it can be seen at Ynys-hir (map 49) between October and April.

whooper swans

shelduck

wigeon

goldeneye

great-crested grebe

red-throated
diver

winter wildfowl

KEY TO MAPS

Roads

Public Footpaths

Forestry Tracks (permissive paths)

Parking   [P]   Information   [i]

Railway Lines and Stations

Buildings

Sand Banks
Mud Flats

Deciduous woodland

Coniferous Forest

Marshland

Sea, Rivers, Estuaries, Lakes

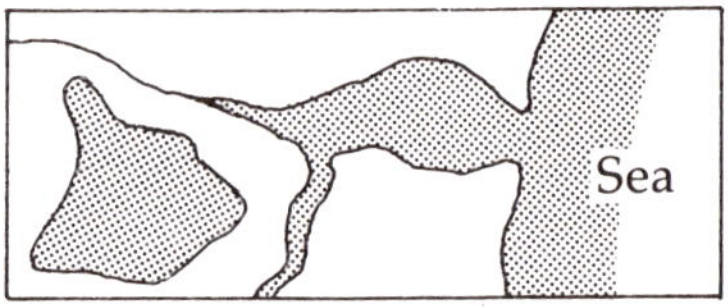

Sea

RSPB Reserve

National Nature Reserve NNR

National Trust

Forestry Commission

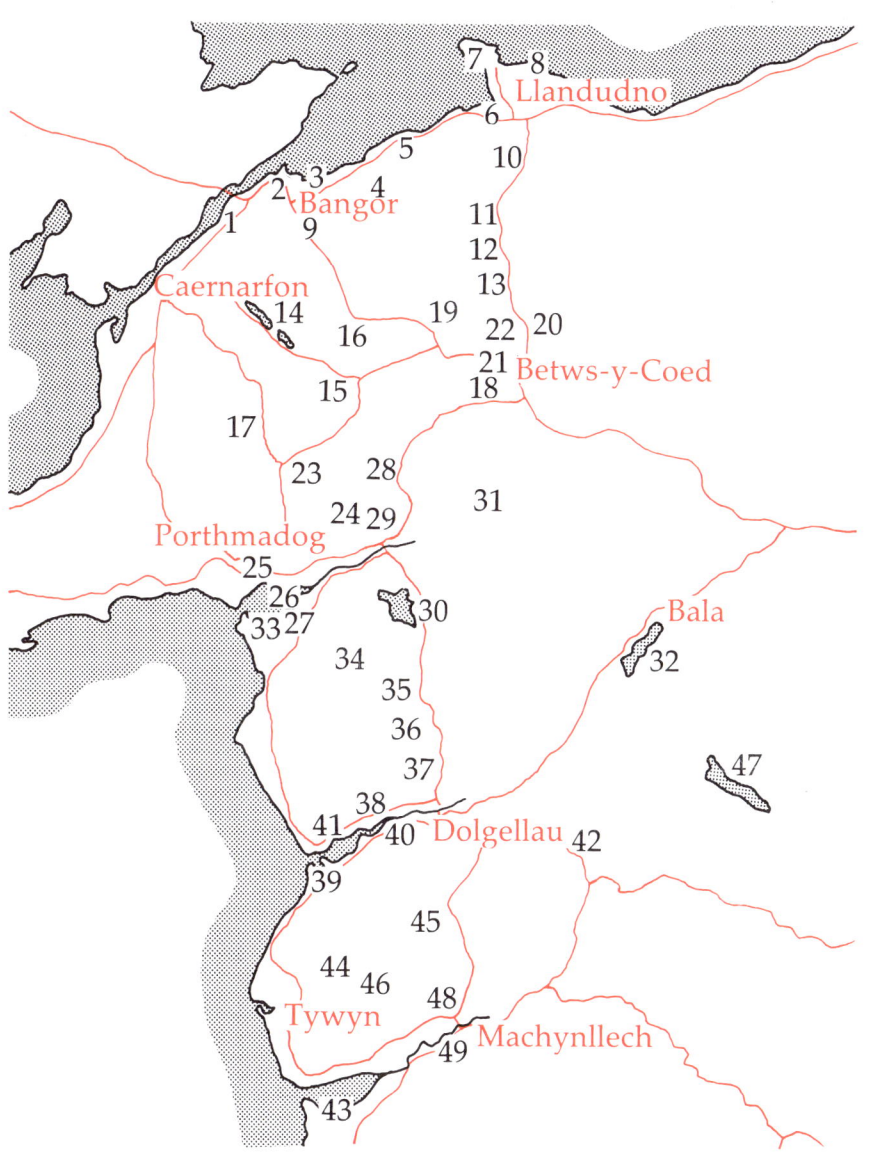

GLAN FAENOL

Access to Glan Faenol is from A487. Find estate entrance 400 yards west of A5 intersection leading onto Britannia Bridge. Open daily, dawn to dusk.

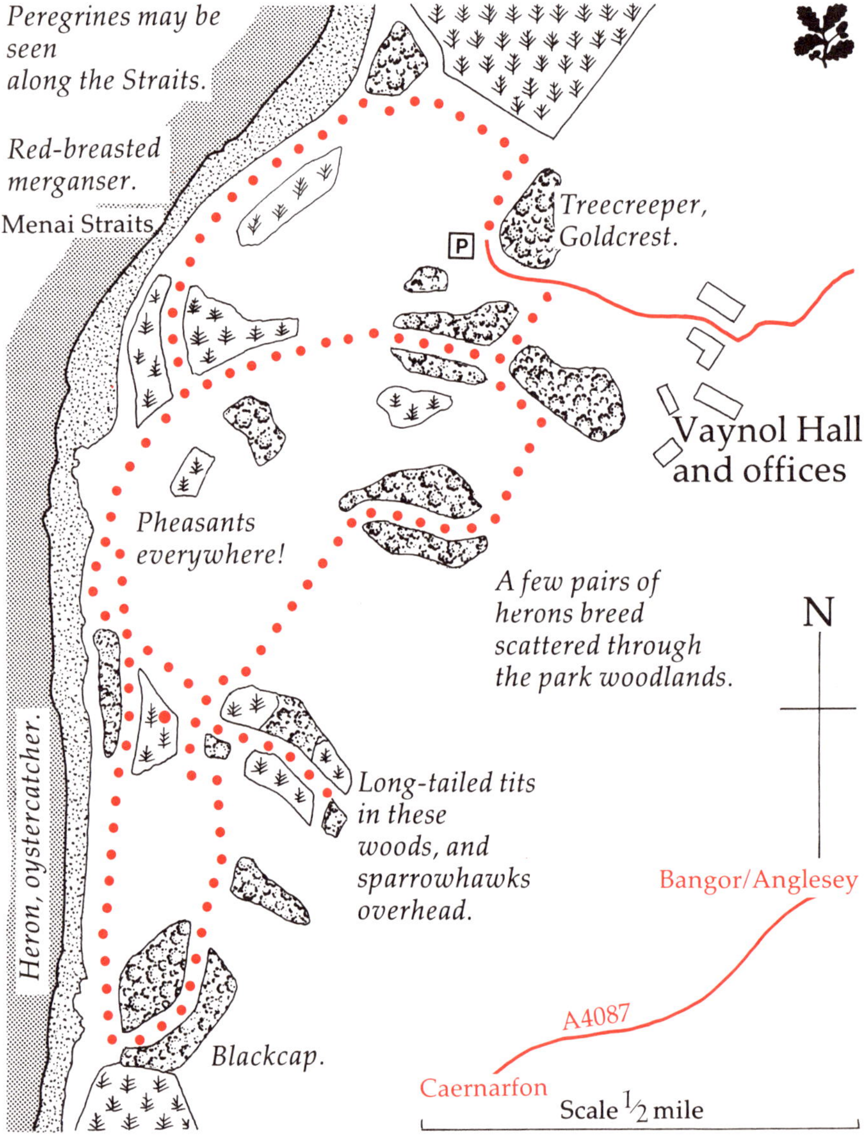

Peregrines may be seen along the Straits.

Red-breasted merganser.

Menai Straits

Treecreeper, Goldcrest.

P

Vaynol Hall and offices

Pheasants everywhere!

A few pairs of herons breed scattered through the park woodlands.

N

Long-tailed tits in these woods, and sparrowhawks overhead.

Bangor/Anglesey

Heron, oystercatcher.

A4087

Blackcap.

Caernarfon

Scale $^1/_2$ mile

BANGOR DOCKS

The A5 passes close to the shore of Bangor harbour on the eastern approach to the city. Ample parking. Excellent views of shore birds.

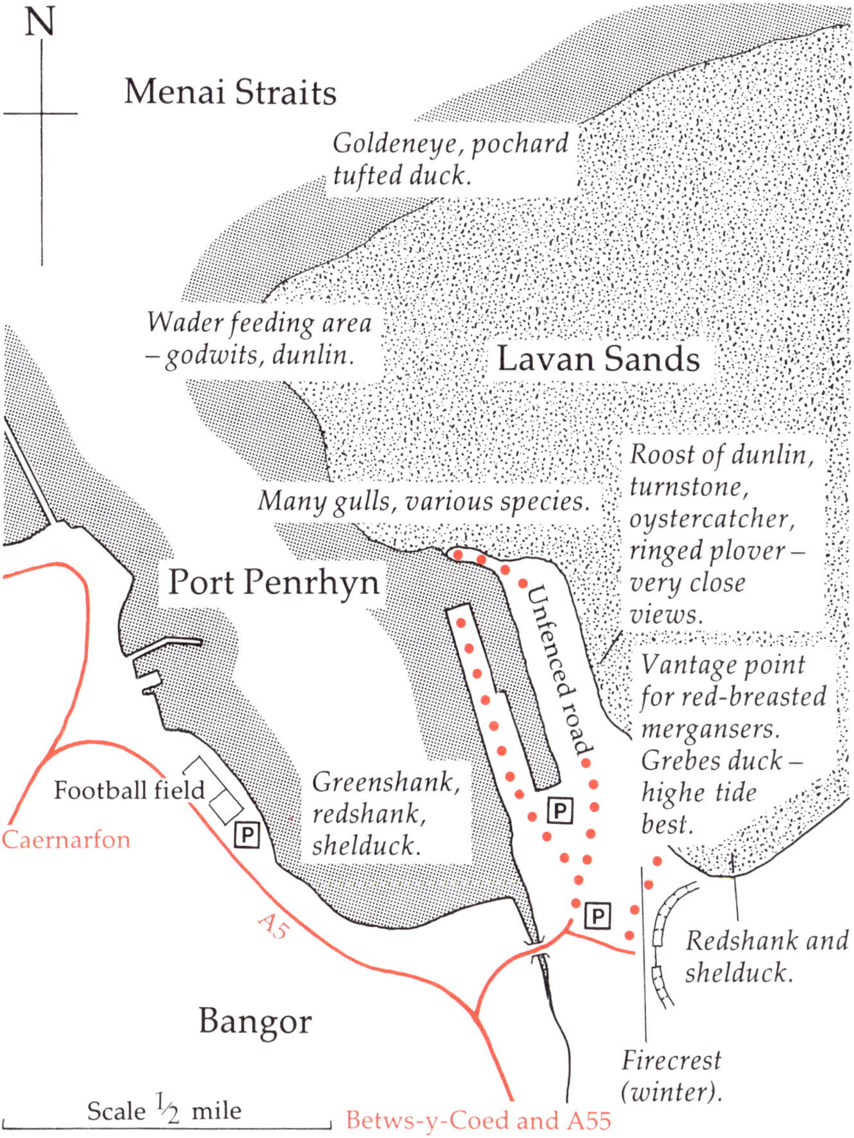

N

Menai Straits

Goldeneye, pochard tufted duck.

Wader feeding area – godwits, dunlin.

Lavan Sands

Roost of dunlin, turnstone, oystercatcher, ringed plover – very close views.

Many gulls, various species.

Port Penrhyn

Unfenced road

Vantage point for red-breasted mergansers. Grebes duck – highe tide best.

Football field

Caernarfon

P

Greenshank, redshank, shelduck.

P

P

Redshank and shelduck.

A5

Bangor

Firecrest (winter).

Scale ½ mile

Betws-y-Coed and A55

2

TRAETH LAFAN

Aber Ogwen is on the south shore of Menai Straits overlooking Traeth Lafan. Access is via the (old) A55 ¼ mile east of Talybont village. Parking on site. N. Wales Naturalist Trust hide at Spinneys. Excellent shore birds.

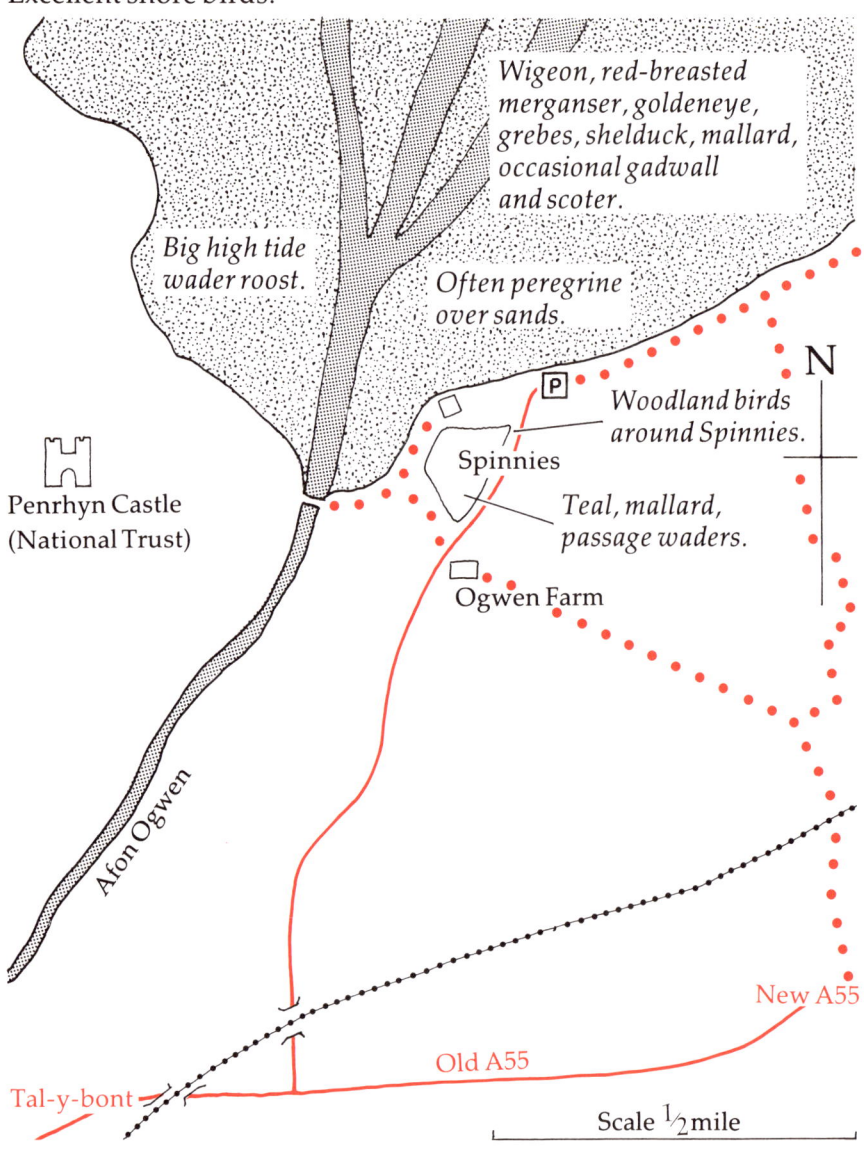

Wigeon, red-breasted merganser, goldeneye, grebes, shelduck, mallard, occasional gadwall and scoter.

Big high tide wader roost.

Often peregrine over sands.

Woodland birds around Spinnies.

Spinnies

N

Penrhyn Castle (National Trust)

Teal, mallard, passage waders.

Ogwen Farm

Afon Ogwen

New A55

Old A55

Tal-y-bont

Scale ½ mile

Turn off A55 in Aber village. Follow through village to Bont Newydd, ¾ mile, to car park. Routes into Aber woods from here.

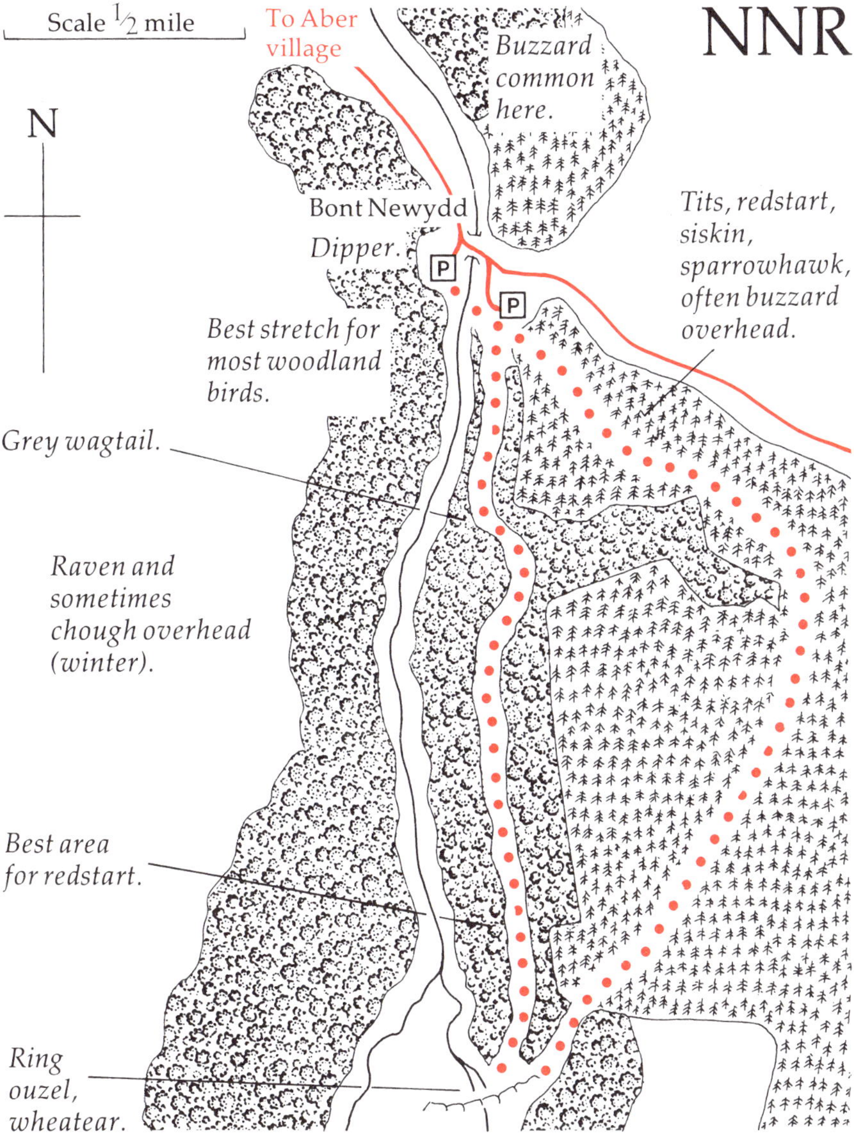

Scale ½ mile

To Aber village

NNR

N

Buzzard common here.

Bont Newydd
Dipper.

Tits, redstart, siskin, sparrowhawk, often buzzard overhead.

Best stretch for most woodland birds.

Grey wagtail.

Raven and sometimes chough overhead (winter).

Best area for redstart.

Ring ouzel, wheatear.

LLANFAIRFECHAN

Halfway between Bangor and Conwy, Llanfairfechan has a good variety of birds; best of all in winter. Access to coast path from prom. or by minor road 1 mile west of village centre.

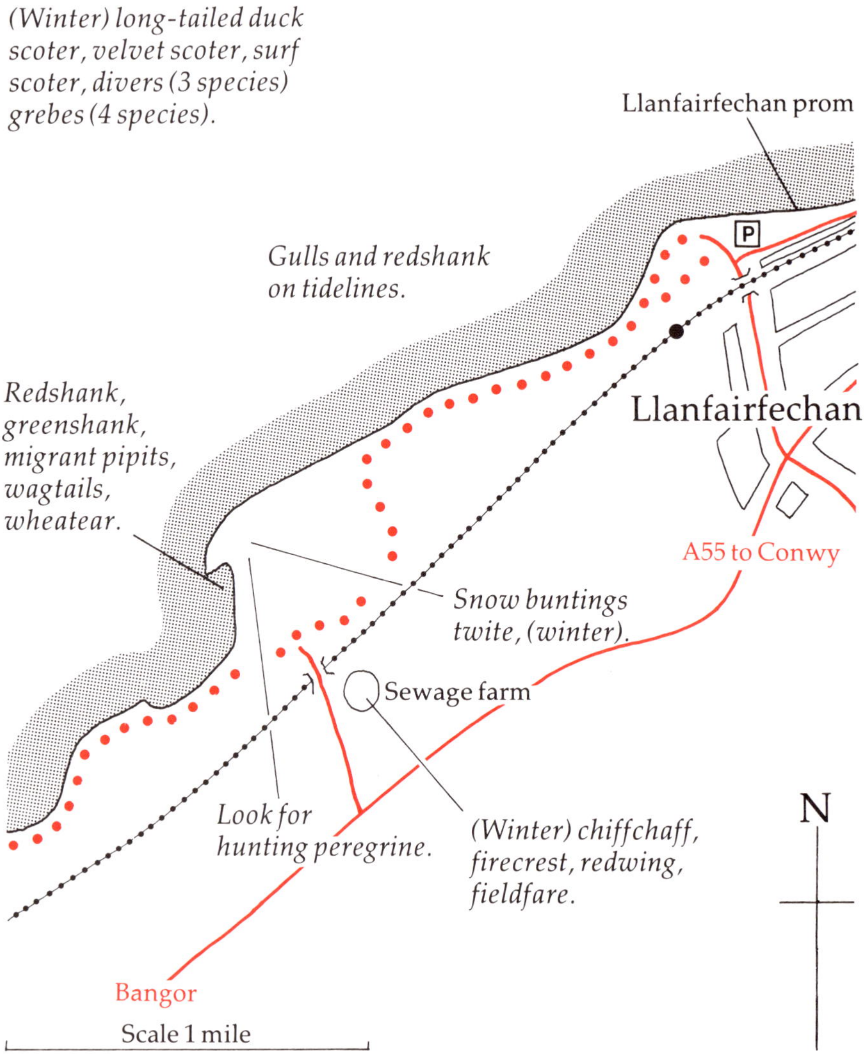

(Winter) long-tailed duck scoter, velvet scoter, surf scoter, divers (3 species) grebes (4 species).

Llanfairfechan prom

P

Gulls and redshank on tidelines.

Redshank, greenshank, migrant pipits, wagtails, wheatear.

Llanfairfechan

A55 to Conwy

Snow buntings twite, (winter).

Sewage farm

N

Look for hunting peregrine.

(Winter) chiffchaff, firecrest, redwing, fieldfare.

Bangor

Scale 1 mile

MORFA CONWY

Conwy sands and estuary are important for wintering waders and wildfowl. Binoculars essential; telescope desirable. Easy walking on coast path or sands.
View from east (Deganwy) side.

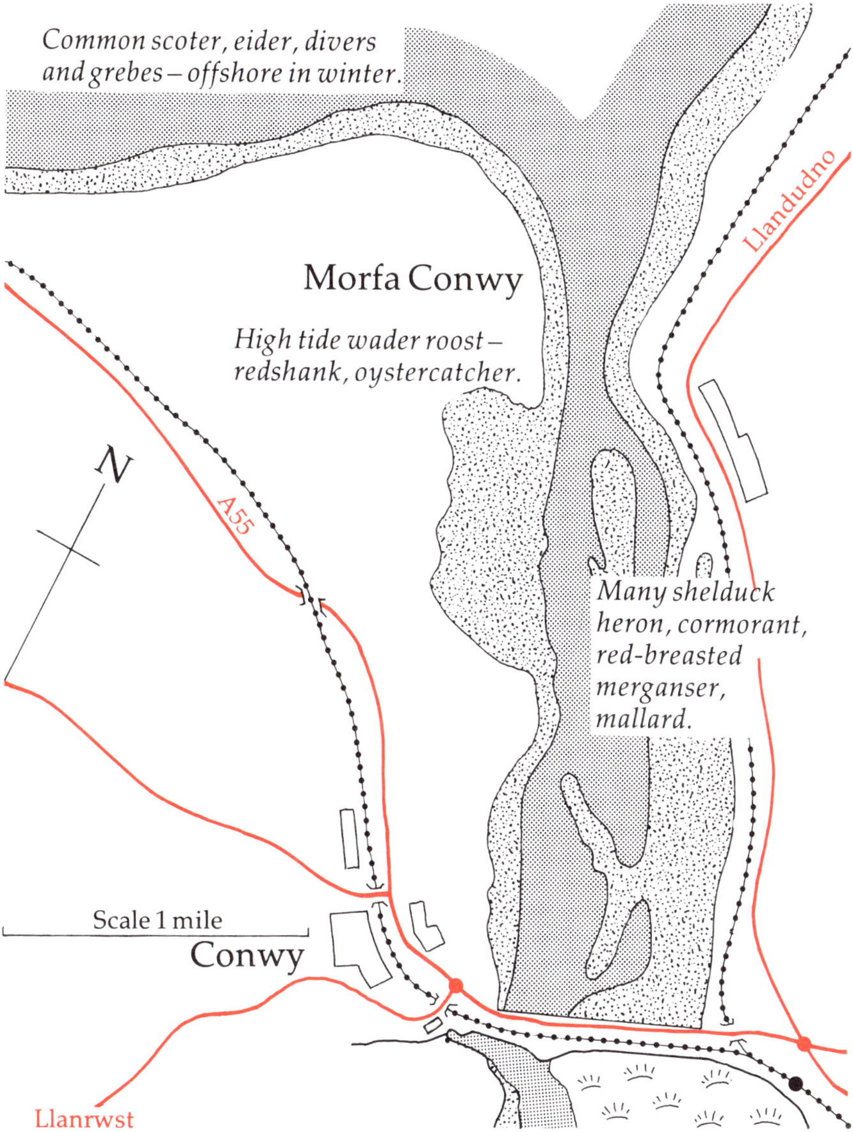

Common scoter, eider, divers and grebes – offshore in winter.

Morfa Conwy

High tide wader roost – redshank, oystercatcher.

Llandudno

N

A55

Many shelduck heron, cormorant, red-breasted merganser, mallard.

Scale 1 mile

Conwy

Llanrwst

6

Take the toll road from Llandudno on to Great Orme. Ample parking areas. Easy walking.

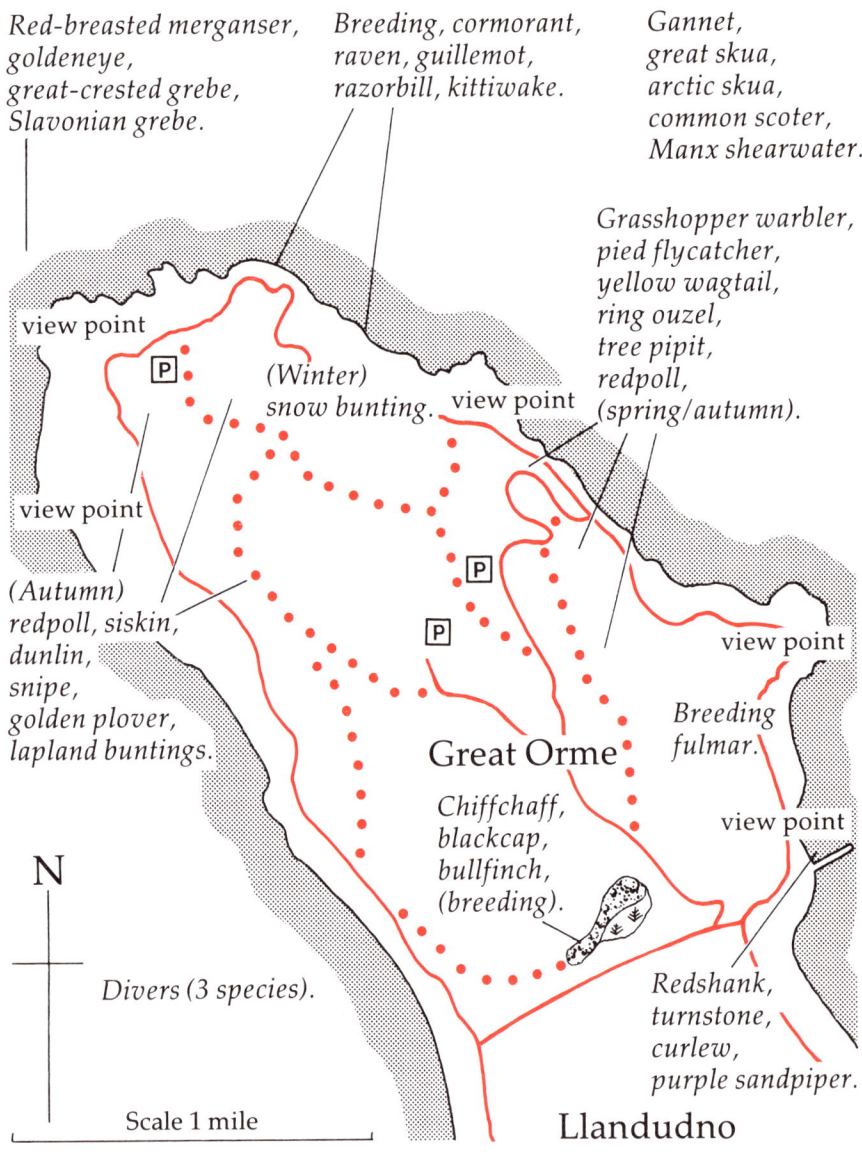

Red-breasted merganser, goldeneye, great-crested grebe, Slavonian grebe.

Breeding, cormorant, raven, guillemot, razorbill, kittiwake.

Gannet, great skua, arctic skua, common scoter, Manx shearwater.

Grasshopper warbler, pied flycatcher, yellow wagtail, ring ouzel, tree pipit, redpoll, (spring/autumn).

view point

view point

(Winter) snow bunting.

view point

view point

view point

(Autumn) redpoll, siskin, dunlin, snipe, golden plover, lapland buntings.

Breeding fulmar.

Great Orme

Chiffchaff, blackcap, bullfinch, (breeding).

view point

N

Divers (3 species).

Redshank, turnstone, curlew, purple sandpiper.

Scale 1 mile

Llandudno

LITTLE ORME

Park at E. end of Llandudno promenade. Good viewpoint here onto breeding colonies. 10 mins. walk to Little Orme itself.

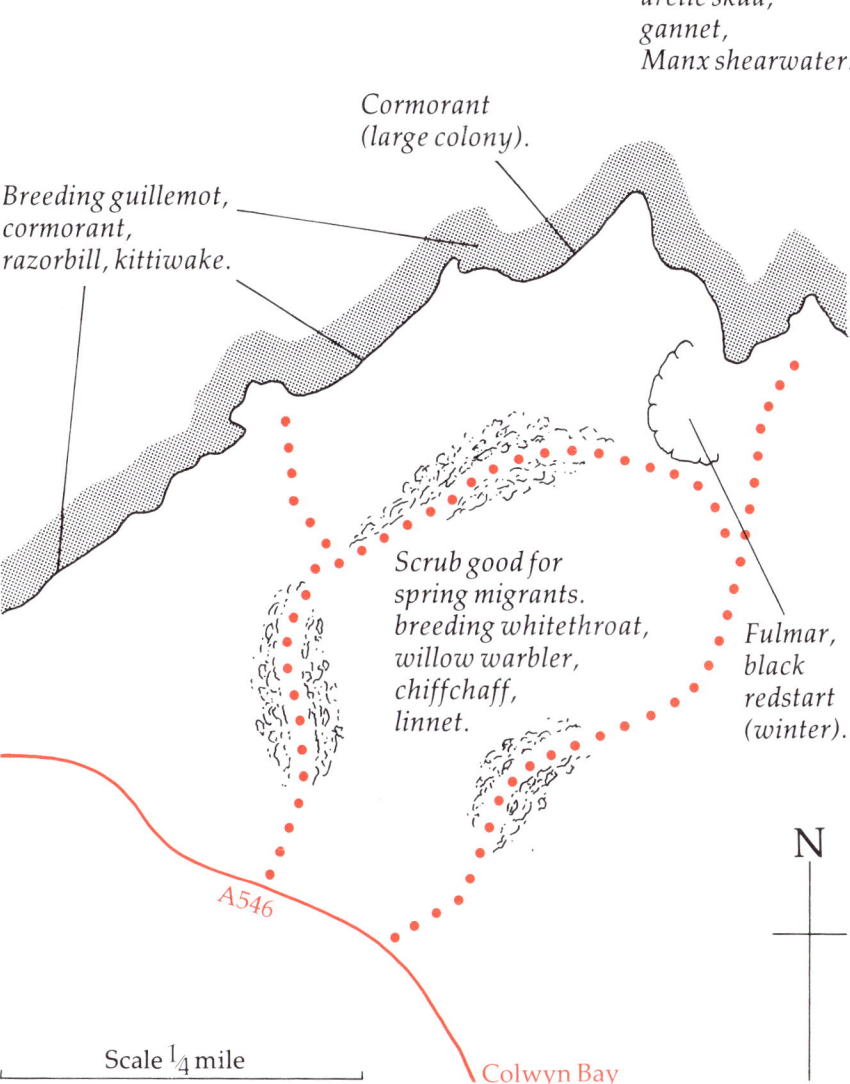

Great skua,
arctic skua,
gannet,
Manx shearwater.

Cormorant
(large colony).

Breeding guillemot,
cormorant,
razorbill, kittiwake.

Scrub good for
spring migrants.
breeding whitethroat,
willow warbler,
chiffchaff,
linnet.

Fulmar,
black
redstart
(winter).

A546

Colwyn Bay

Scale $\frac{1}{4}$ mile

N

HALFWAY BRIDGE

Halfway Bridge is the bridge over Afon Ogwen between Bethesda and Bangor. Limited parking. Superb river for water birds.

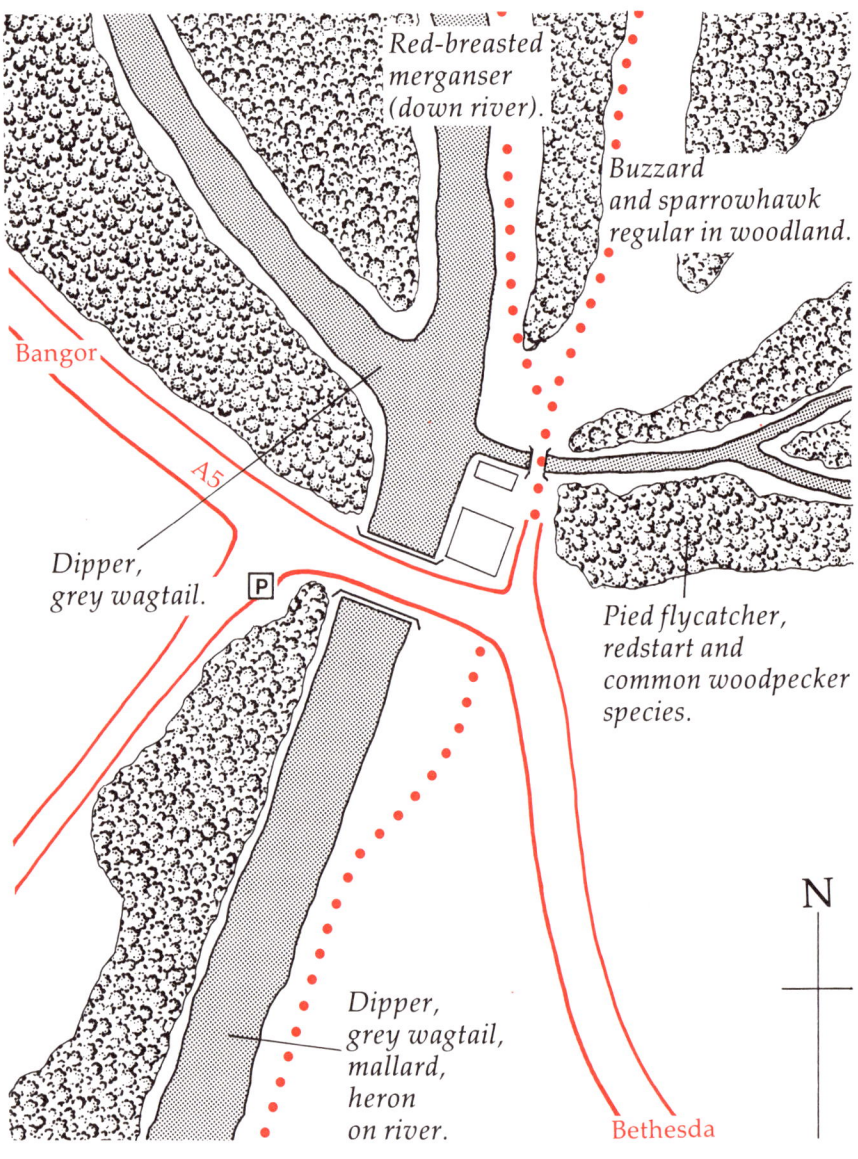

Red-breasted merganser (down river).

Buzzard and sparrowhawk regular in woodland.

Bangor

A5

Dipper, grey wagtail.

P

Pied flycatcher, redstart and common woodpecker species.

N

Dipper, grey wagtail, mallard, heron on river.

Bethesda

Lower Conwy estuary between Glan Conwy and the Conwy bridge.
Good vantage points on A470 between Llanwrst and Llandudno
Junction. Limited roadside parking.

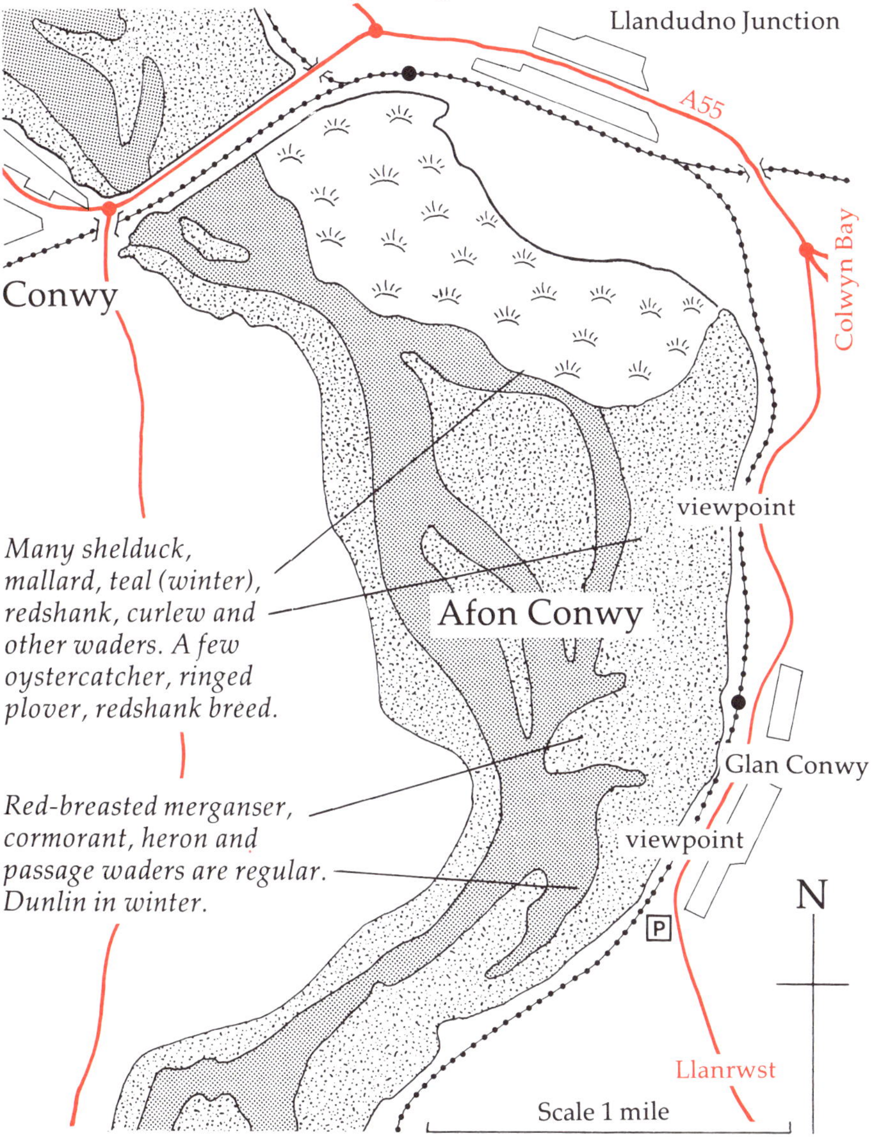

Llandudno Junction

A55

Colwyn Bay

Conwy

viewpoint

*Many shelduck,
mallard, teal (winter),
redshank, curlew and
other waders. A few
oystercatcher, ringed
plover, redshank breed.*

Afon Conwy

*Red-breasted merganser,
cormorant, heron and
passage waders are regular.
Dunlin in winter.*

Glan Conwy

viewpoint

N

P

Llanrwst

Scale 1 mile

Tal-y-Cafn village is on the A470 between Llanwrst and Glan Conwy. The river bridge and its environs give excellent views upstream and downstream on Afon Conwy.

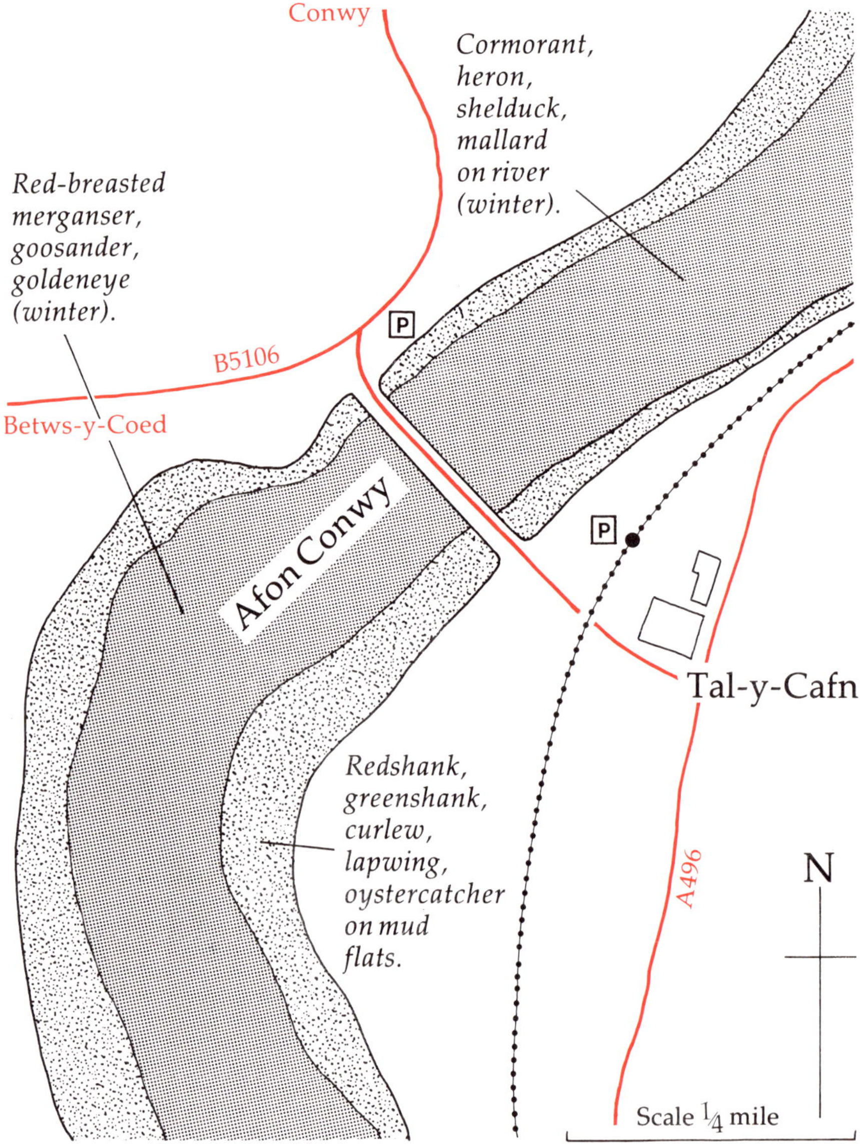

Conwy

Cormorant, heron, shelduck, mallard on river (winter).

Red-breasted merganser, goosander, goldeneye (winter).

B5106

Betws-y-Coed

P

P

Afon Conwy

Tal-y-Cafn

Redshank, greenshank, curlew, lapwing, oystercatcher on mud flats.

A496

N

Scale ¹⁄₄ mile

CAERHUN CHURCHYARD

Caerhun is on the west side of Afon Conwy on B5106 between Dolgarrog (2 miles) and Conwy. Caerhun churchyard is the most reliable place in Snowdonia to find hawfinch. Many other bird species around Roman Fort.

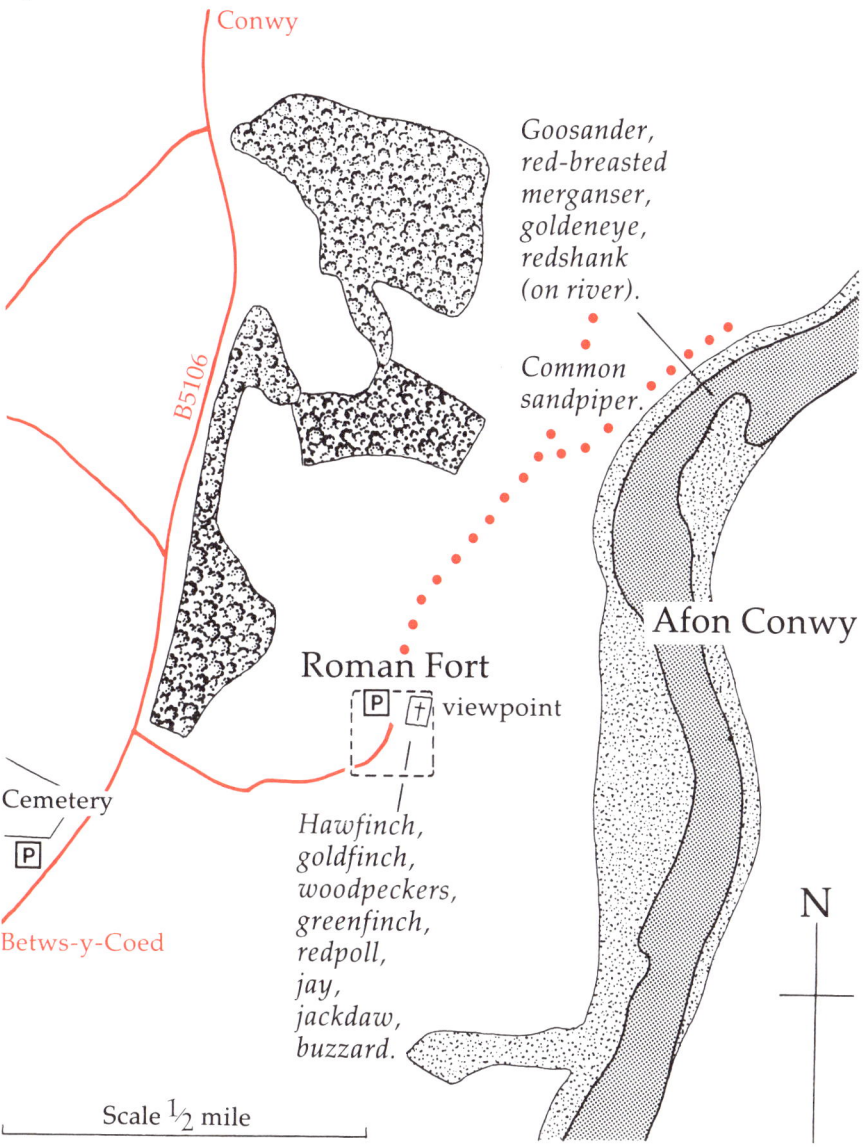

Conwy

Goosander, red-breasted merganser, goldeneye, redshank (on river).

Common sandpiper.

B5106

Afon Conwy

Roman Fort

P † viewpoint

Cemetery

P

Betws-y-Coed

Hawfinch, goldfinch, woodpeckers, greenfinch, redpoll, jay, jackdaw, buzzard.

N

Scale ½ mile

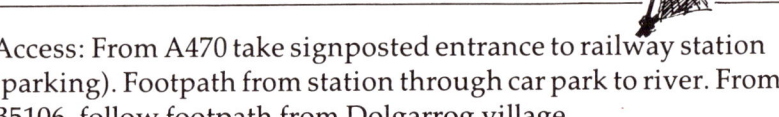

Access: From A470 take signposted entrance to railway station (parking). Footpath from station through car park to river. From B5106, follow footpath from Dolgarrog village.

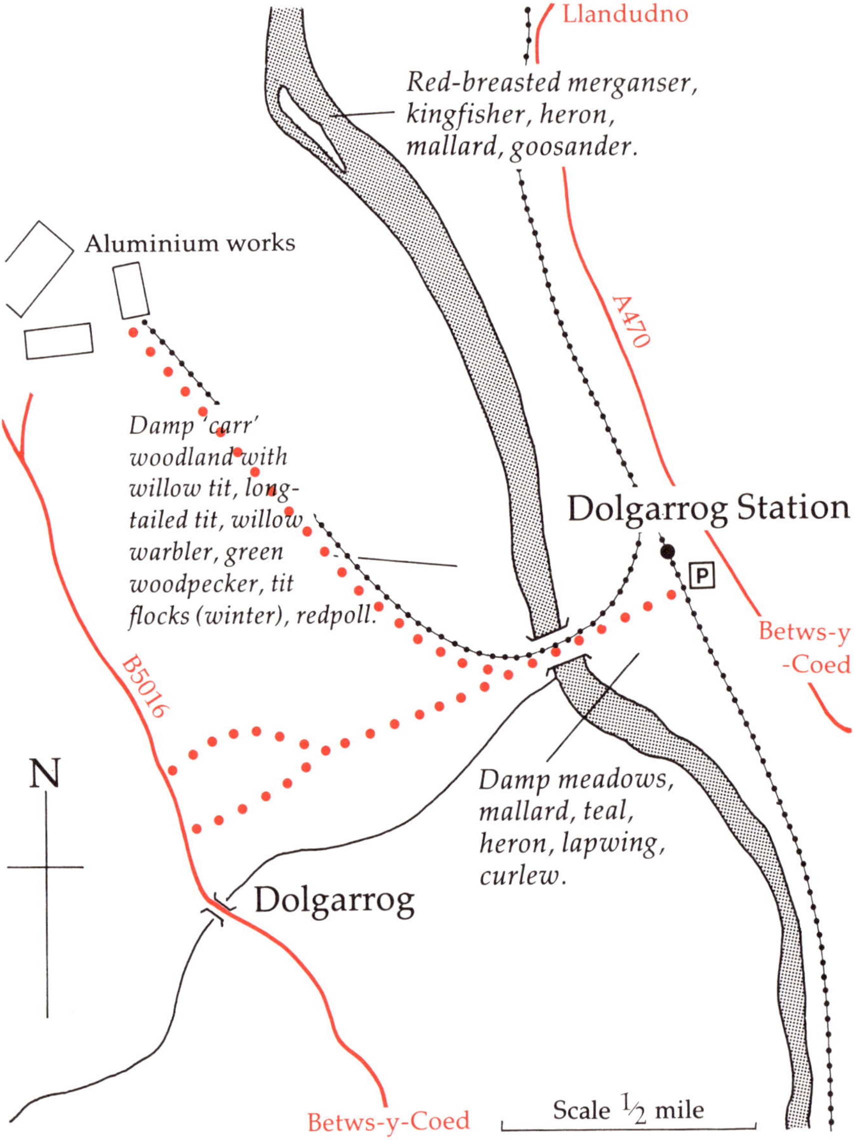

Llandudno

Red-breasted merganser, kingfisher, heron, mallard, goosander.

A470

Aluminium works

Damp 'carr' woodland with willow tit, long-tailed tit, willow warbler, green woodpecker, tit flocks (winter), redpoll.

B5016

Dolgarrog Station

P

Betws-y-Coed

N

Damp meadows, mallard, teal, heron, lapwing, curlew.

Dolgarrog

Betws-y-Coed

Scale ½ mile

PADARN COUNTRY PARK

Padarn Country Park: signposted in Llanberis.
Ample parking. Well marked woodland trails. Approach Dinorwic
quarries from top via lanes from Deiniolen (good parking and
paths) or via tracks from Country Park.

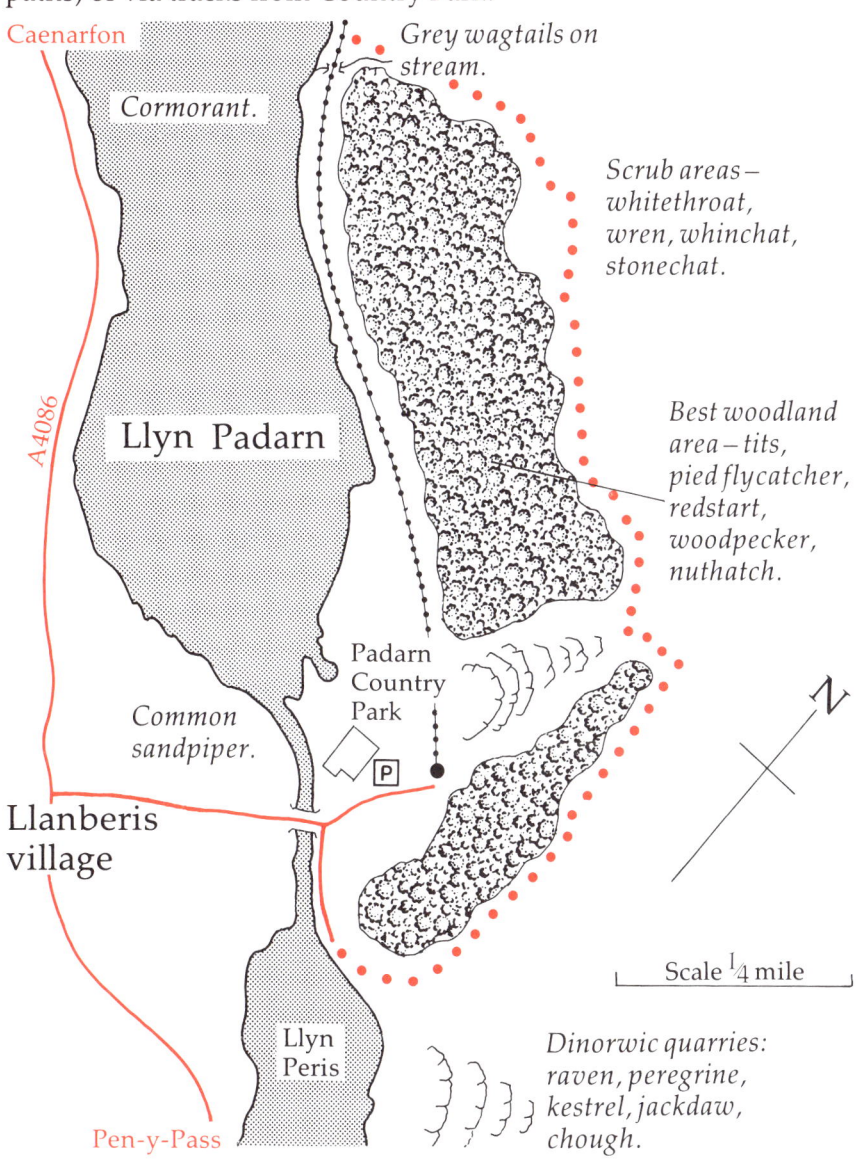

Caenarfon

Cormorant.

Grey wagtails on stream.

Scrub areas –
whitethroat,
wren, whinchat,
stonechat.

A4086

Llyn Padarn

Best woodland
area – tits,
pied flycatcher,
redstart,
woodpecker,
nuthatch.

Padarn
Country
Park

Common
sandpiper.

P

Llanberis
village

N

Scale ¹⁄4 mile

Llyn
Peris

Pen-y-Pass

Dinorwic quarries:
raven, peregrine,
kestrel, jackdaw,
chough.

MINERS' TRACK

For Dinas Mot, park in layby at Pont-y-Cromlech.
Park at Pen-y-Pass for start of Miners' Track to Snowdon summit. Be
properly equipped for Snowdon walk! Beware poor weather
conditions!

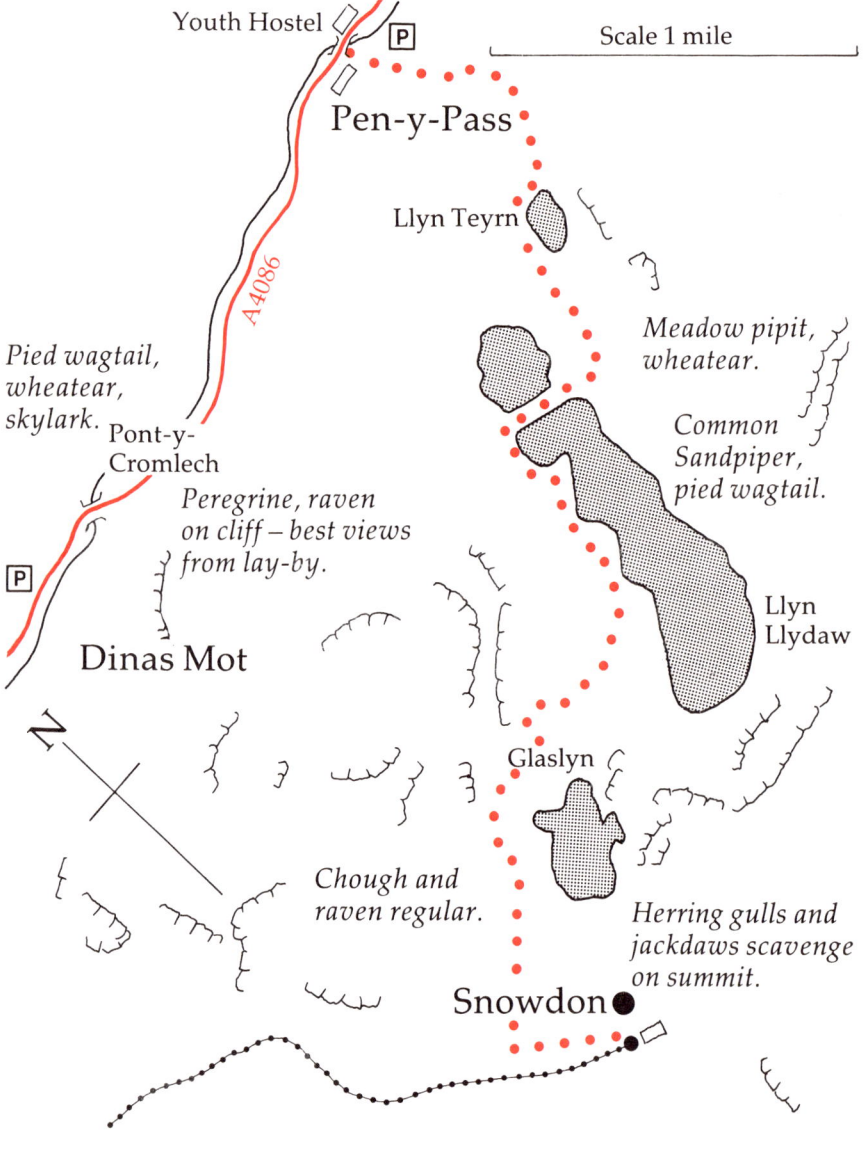

Youth Hostel

Pen-y-Pass

P

Scale 1 mile

Llyn Teyrn

A4086

*Pied wagtail,
wheatear,
skylark.*

Pont-y-
Cromlech

*Peregrine, raven
on cliff – best views
from lay-by.*

Dinas Mot

N

*Meadow pipit,
wheatear.*

*Common
Sandpiper,
pied wagtail.*

Llyn
Llydaw

Glaslyn

*Chough and
raven regular.*

*Herring gulls and
jackdaws scavenge
on summit.*

Snowdon

Park near Idwal Cottage Youth Hostel at west end of Llyn Ogwen on A5, 4 miles N. of Bethesda. Path to Cwm Idwal starts from the car park.

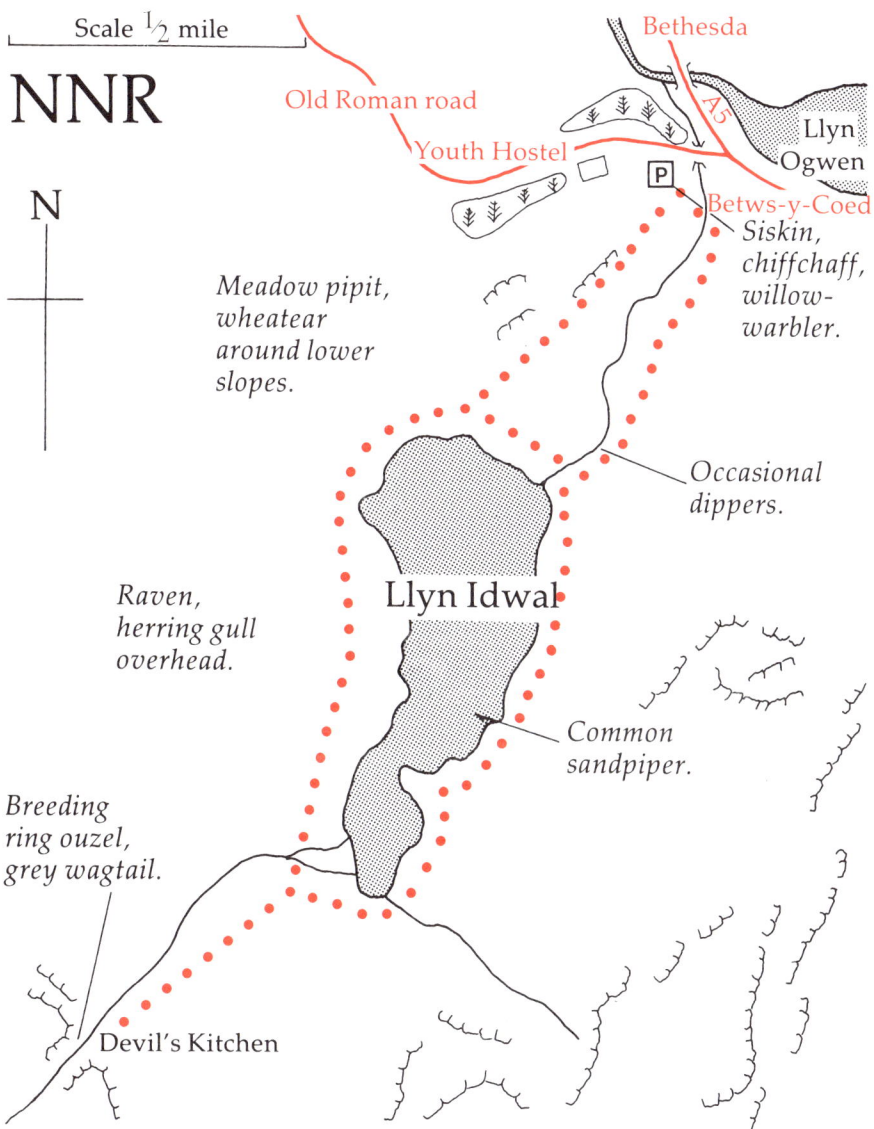

Scale ½ mile

NNR

N

Old Roman road

Bethesda

Youth Hostel

A5

Llyn Ogwen

P

Betws-y-Coed

Siskin, chiffchaff, willow-warbler.

Meadow pipit, wheatear around lower slopes.

Occasional dippers.

Llyn Idwal

Raven, herring gull overhead.

Common sandpiper.

Breeding ring ouzel, grey wagtail.

Devil's Kitchen

LLYN-Y-GADAIR

Llyn-y-Gadair is on the west side of A4085 (Caernarfon-Beddgelert) by the hamlet of Rhyd Ddu.

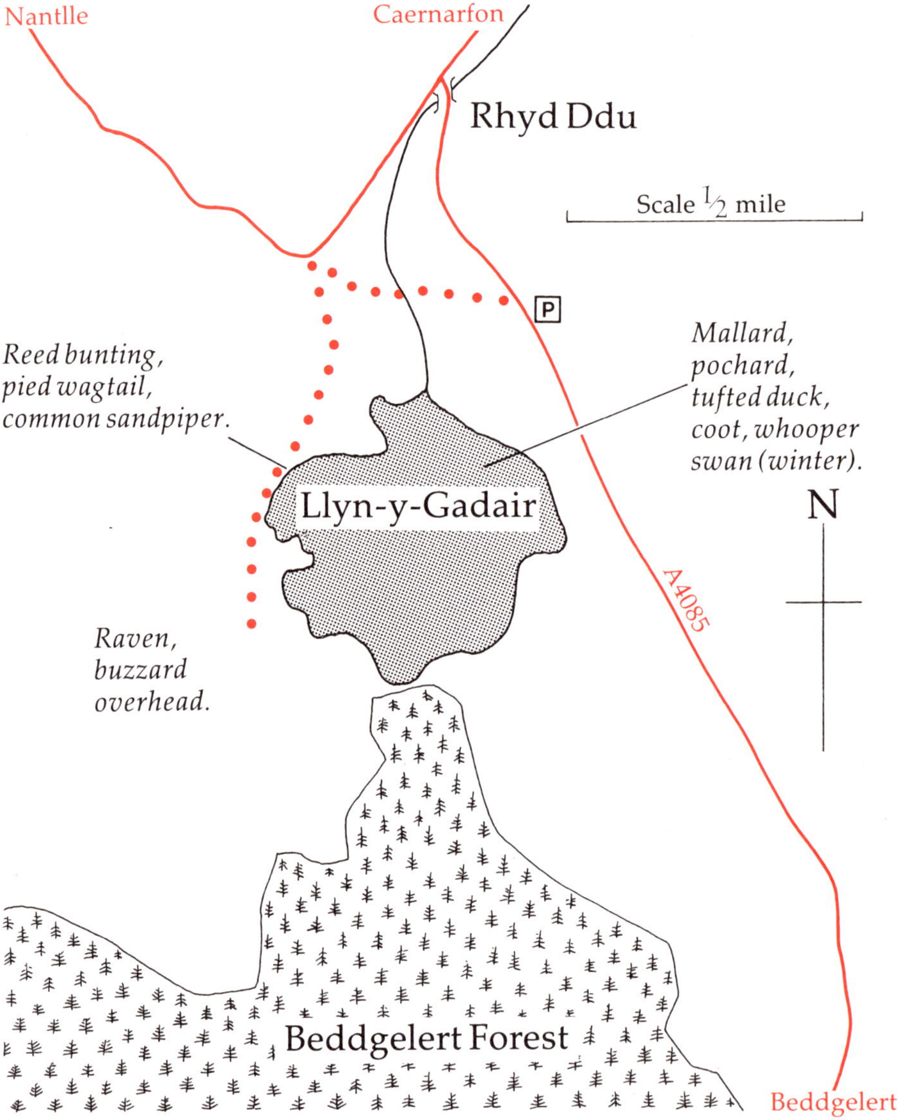

Nantlle

Caernarfon

Rhyd Ddu

Scale $^{1}/_{2}$ mile

P

Reed bunting,
pied wagtail,
common sandpiper.

Mallard,
pochard,
tufted duck,
coot, whooper
swan (winter).

Llyn-y-Gadair

N

A4085

Raven,
buzzard
overhead.

Beddgelert Forest

Beddgelert

LLYN ELSI

The walk to Llyn Elsi starts from behind the church in Betws-y-Coed and passes through fine conifer and deciduous woodland.

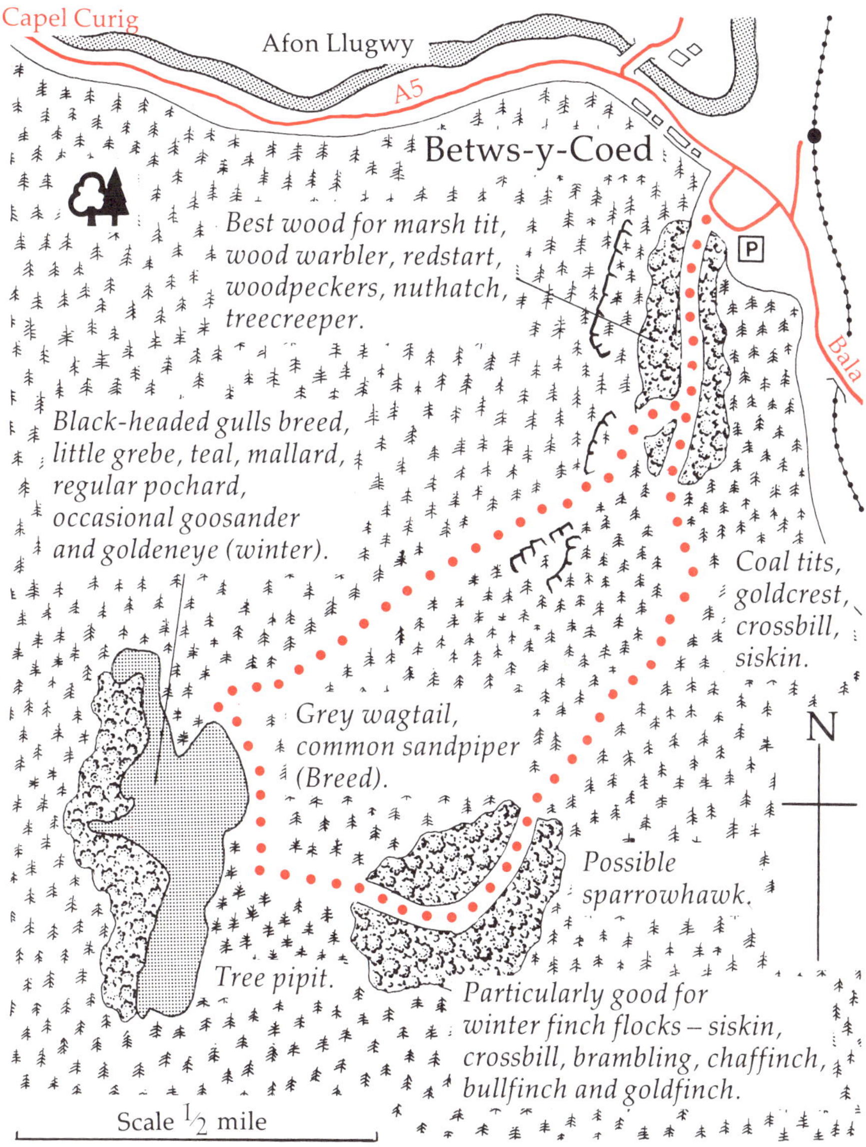

Capel Curig

Afon Llugwy

A5

Betws-y-Coed

P

Bala

Best wood for marsh tit, wood warbler, redstart, woodpeckers, nuthatch, treecreeper.

Black-headed gulls breed, little grebe, teal, mallard, regular pochard, occasional goosander and goldeneye (winter).

Coal tits, goldcrest, crossbill, siskin.

Grey wagtail, common sandpiper (Breed).

N

Possible sparrowhawk.

Tree pipit.

Particularly good for winter finch flocks – siskin, crossbill, brambling, chaffinch, bullfinch and goldfinch.

Scale ½ mile

LLYN GLANGORS

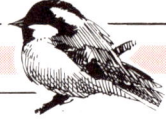

Llyn Glangors trails start from GR SH 771588 on the minor road between the Ugly House on A5 and Llanwrst. Trails lead through varied forest to the beautiful lake on the edge of open moorland.

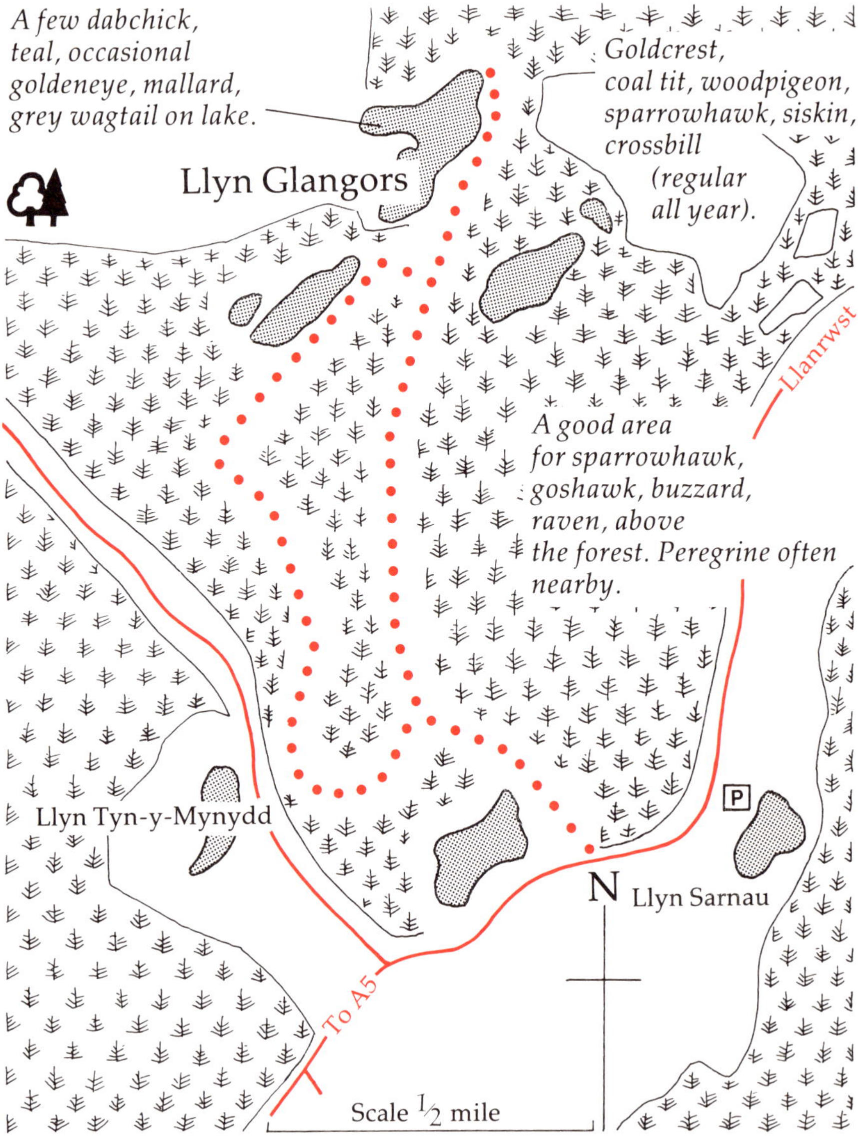

A few dabchick, teal, occasional goldeneye, mallard, grey wagtail on lake.
Llyn Glangors
Goldcrest, coal tit, woodpigeon, sparrowhawk, siskin, crossbill (regular all year).
Llanrwst
A good area for sparrowhawk, goshawk, buzzard, raven, above the forest. Peregrine often nearby.
Llyn Tyn-y-Mynydd
P
N
Llyn Sarnau
To A5
Scale 1/2 mile

COED HAFOD

Coed Hafod at Betws-y-Coed (Llanwrst – Conwy road) is an excellent oak woodland with a full range of Welsh woodland birds. Signposted public footpaths from parking areas on road.

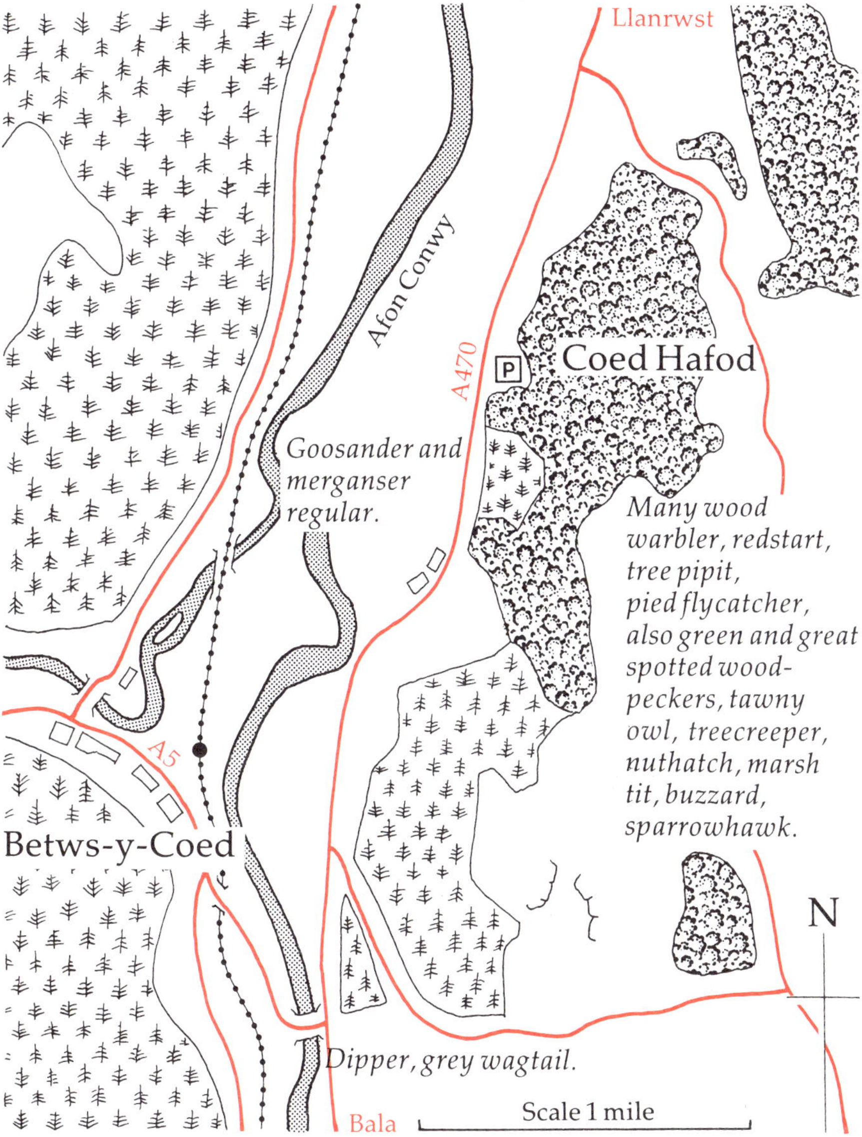

Llanrwst

Afon Conwy

A470

P Coed Hafod

Goosander and merganser regular.

Many wood warbler, redstart, tree pipit, pied flycatcher, also green and great spotted wood-peckers, tawny owl, treecreeper, nuthatch, marsh tit, buzzard, sparrowhawk.

A5

Betws-y-Coed

N

Dipper, grey wagtail.

Bala

Scale 1 mile

The Miners' Bridge walk is a short, easy walk starting right in the centre of Betws-y-Coed village. Fine riverside walk with good birds.

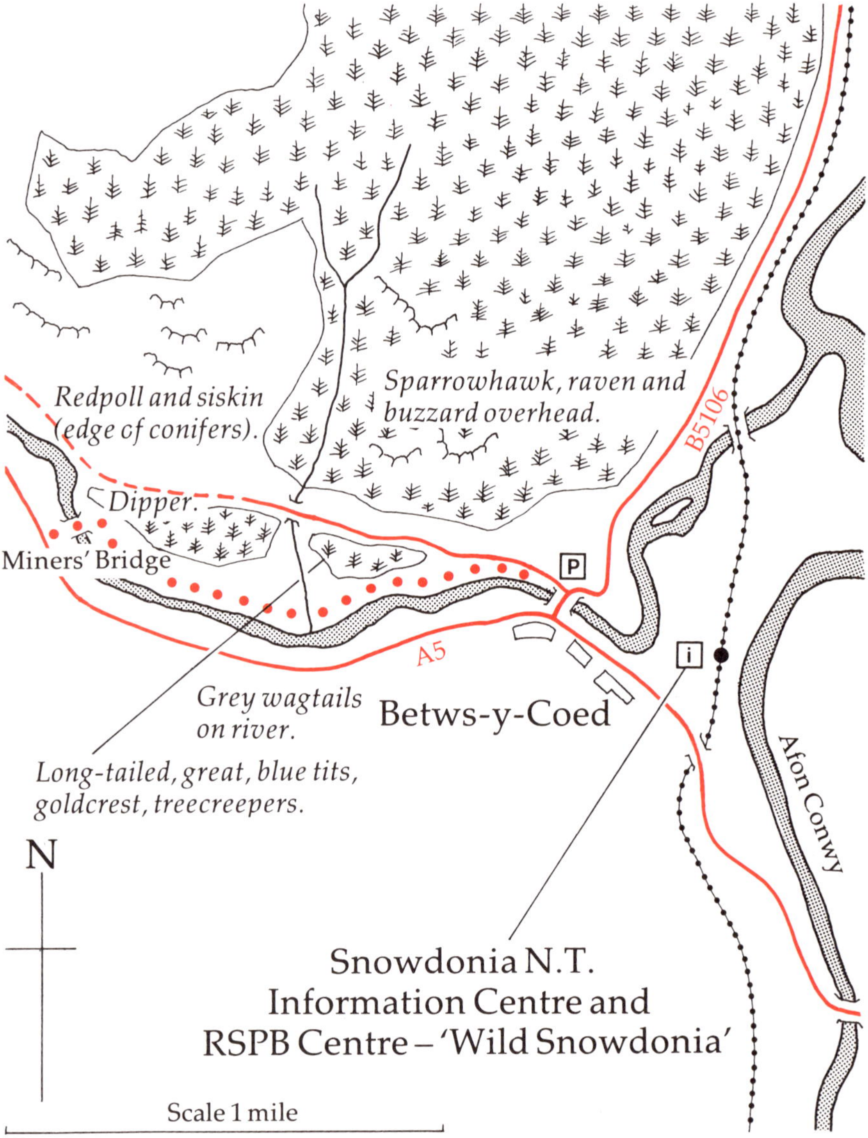

Redpoll and siskin (edge of conifers).

Sparrowhawk, raven and buzzard overhead.

Dipper.

Miners' Bridge

B5106

P

i

A5

Grey wagtails on river.

Betws-y-Coed

Long-tailed, great, blue tits, goldcrest, treecreepers.

Afon Conwy

N

Snowdonia N.T.
Information Centre and
RSPB Centre – 'Wild Snowdonia'

Scale 1 mile

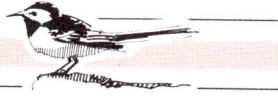

In Betws-y-Coed cross Pont-y-Pair Bridge (car parking),
turn left and then first right (250 yards). Follow ORANGE markers to
Llyn-y-Parc. Varied woodlands, many
birds, spectacular views.

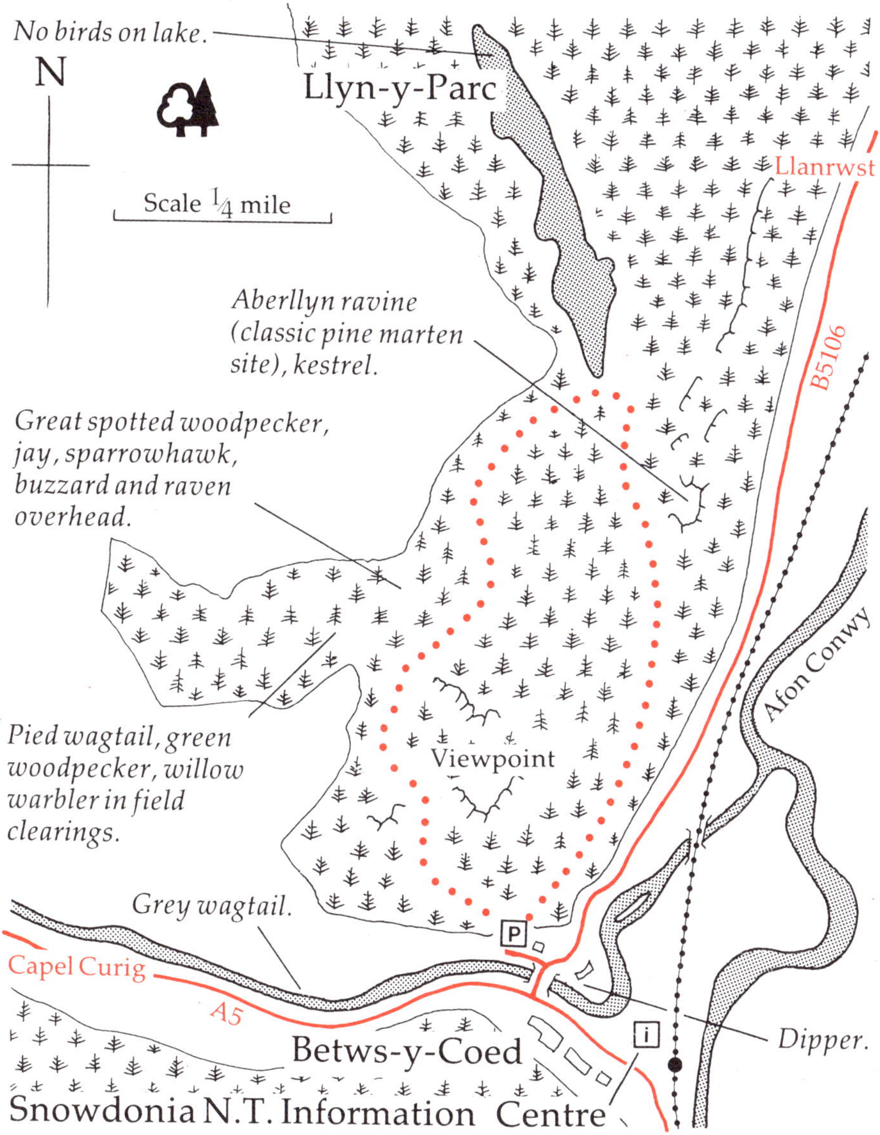

No birds on lake.

N

Llyn-y-Parc

Llanrwst

Scale $^1/_4$ mile

B5106

*Aberllyn ravine
(classic pine marten
site), kestrel.*

*Great spotted woodpecker,
jay, sparrowhawk,
buzzard and raven
overhead.*

Afon Conwy

*Pied wagtail, green
woodpecker, willow
warbler in field
clearings.*

Viewpoint

Grey wagtail.

P

Capel Curig

A5

Betws-y-Coed

i

Dipper.

Snowdonia N.T. Information Centre

ABERGLASLYN PASS

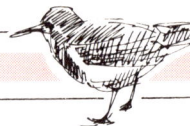

Alternative walks in Aberglaslyn/Beddgelert area. Spectacular views, ample parking. River, woodland and open hillside. Wide variety of birds and good moorland plants.

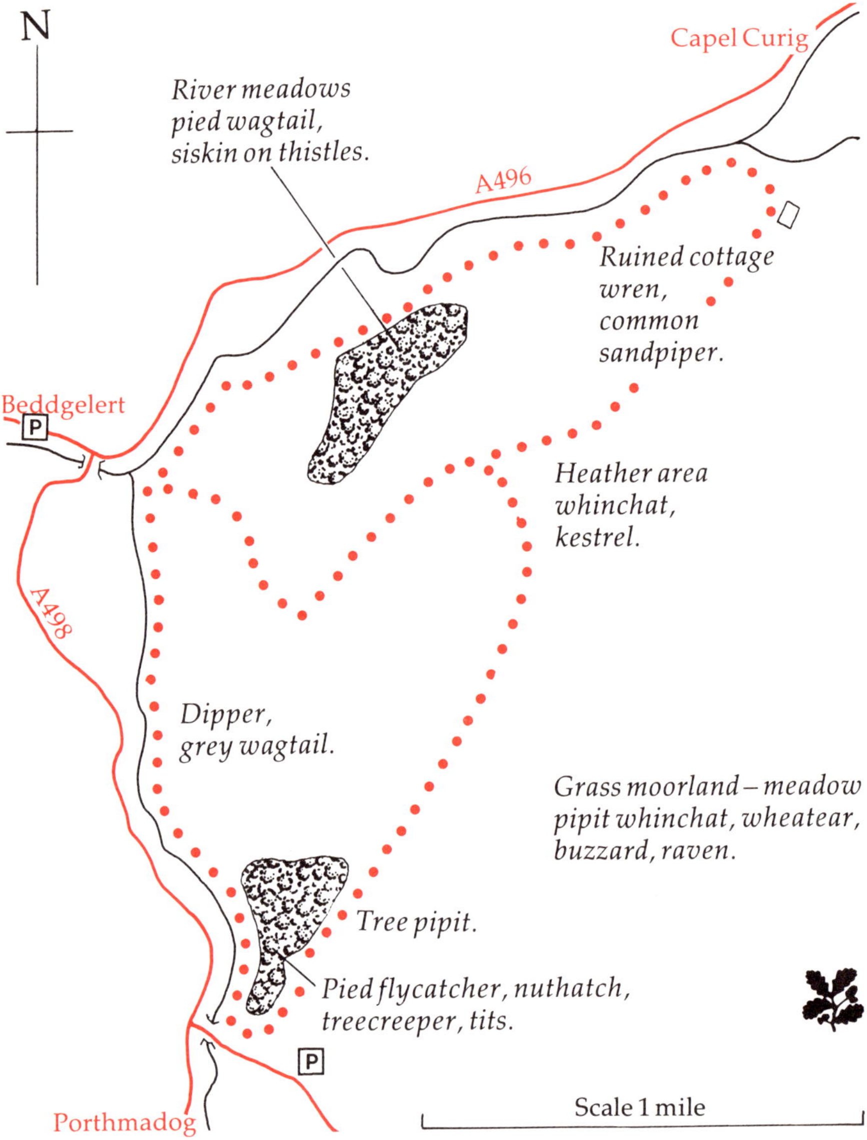

N
Capel Curig
River meadows pied wagtail, siskin on thistles.
A496
Ruined cottage wren, common sandpiper.
Beddgelert
P
Heather area whinchat, kestrel.
A498
Dipper, grey wagtail.
Grass moorland – meadow pipit whinchat, wheatear, buzzard, raven.
Tree pipit.
Pied flycatcher, nuthatch, treecreeper, tits.
P
Porthmadog
Scale 1 mile

CROESOR CNICHT

Croesor is a tiny hamlet (GR SH632446) between Penrhyndeudraeth and Beddgelert. Cnicht is the distinctive pointed mountain behind it. Note: this area is hard walking on very rugged and steep ground.

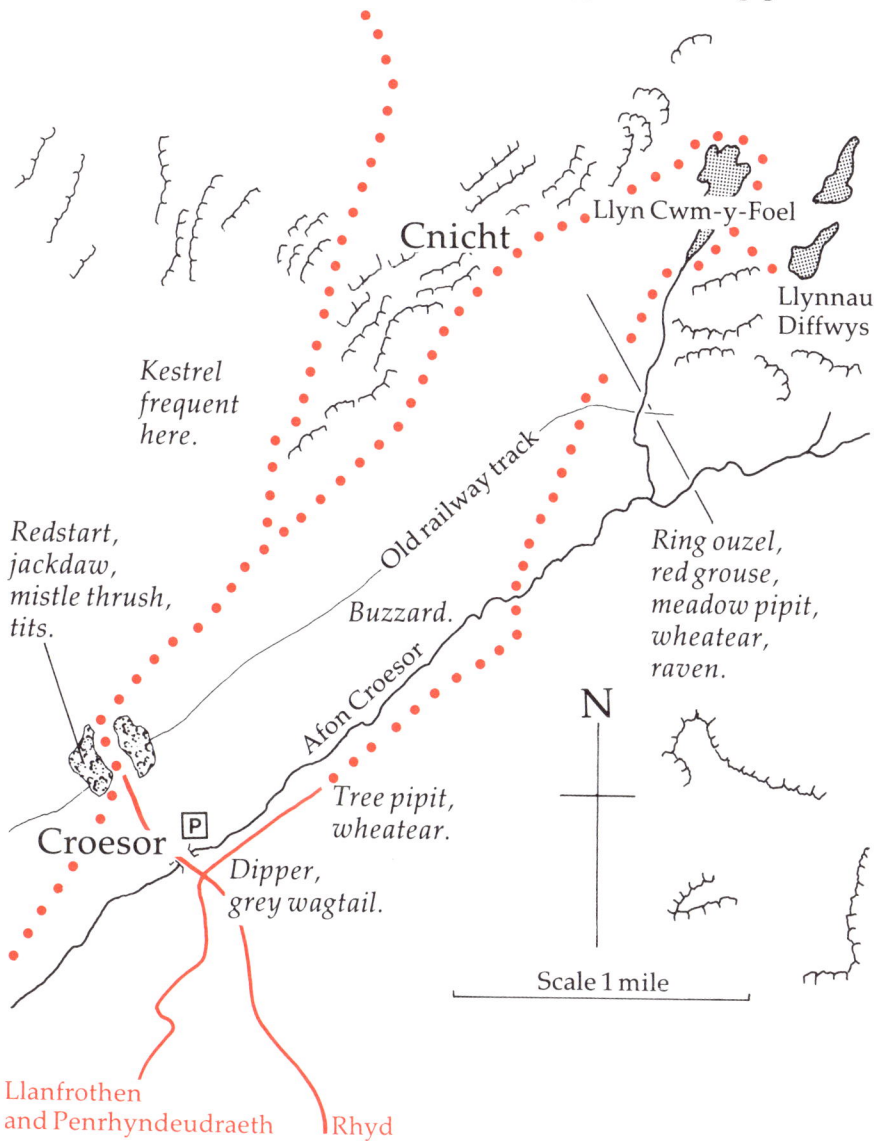

Cnicht

Llyn Cwm-y-Foel

Llynnau Diffwys

Kestrel frequent here.

Redstart, jackdaw, mistle thrush, tits.

Old railway track

Ring ouzel, red grouse, meadow pipit, wheatear, raven.

Buzzard.

Afon Croesor

N

Tree pipit, wheatear.

Croesor

P

Dipper, grey wagtail.

Scale 1 mile

Llanfrothen and Penrhyndeudraeth

Rhyd

24

PORTHMADOG COB

Porthmadog Cob is the road (A487) and railway crossing of Glaslyn Estuary. Good parking near tollgate or in town. Good views of marsh from tollgate lay by.

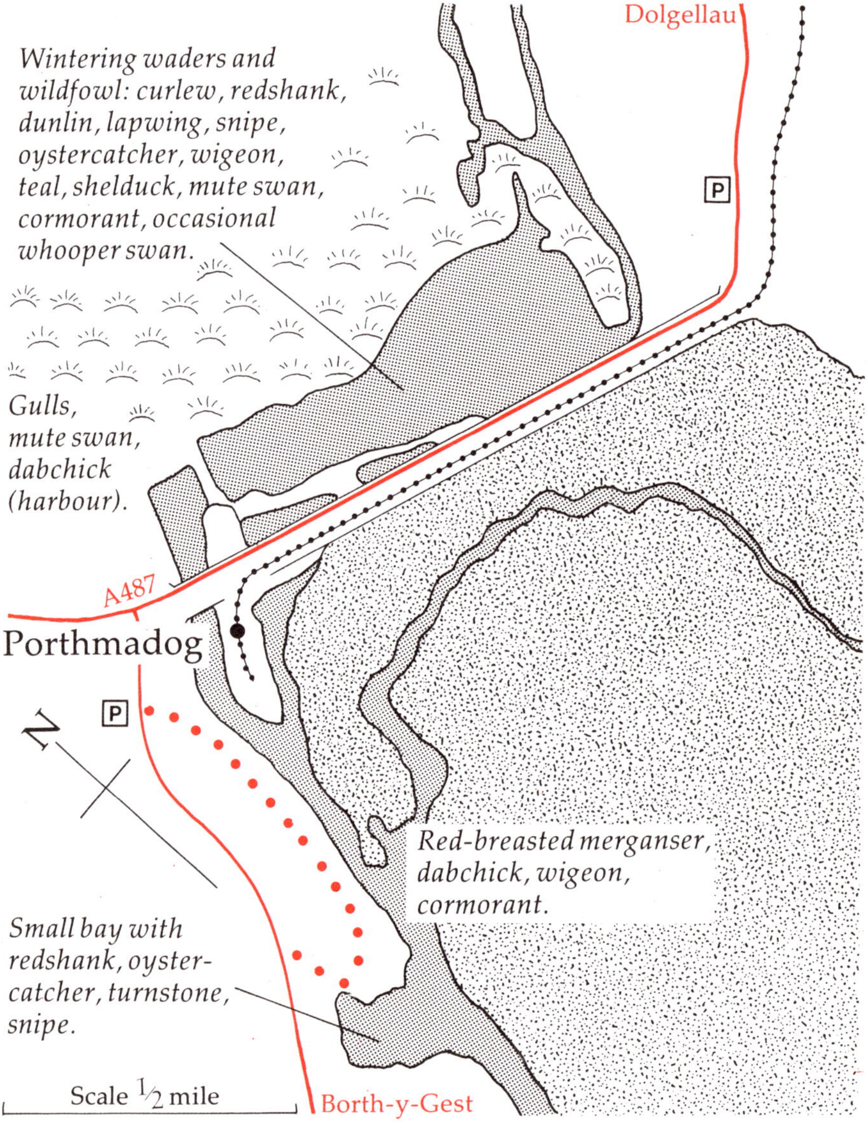

Wintering waders and wildfowl: curlew, redshank, dunlin, lapwing, snipe, oystercatcher, wigeon, teal, shelduck, mute swan, cormorant, occasional whooper swan.

Gulls, mute swan, dabchick (harbour).

Dolgellau

P

A487

Porthmadog

P

N

Red-breasted merganser, dabchick, wigeon, cormorant.

Small bay with redshank, oyster-catcher, turnstone, snipe.

Scale ¹/₂ mile

Borth-y-Gest

PORTMEIRION

The Italian style village at Portmeirion (paid entry) is an experience in itself and the woodlands are splendid for birds. Excellent views of shore in Tremadog Bay.

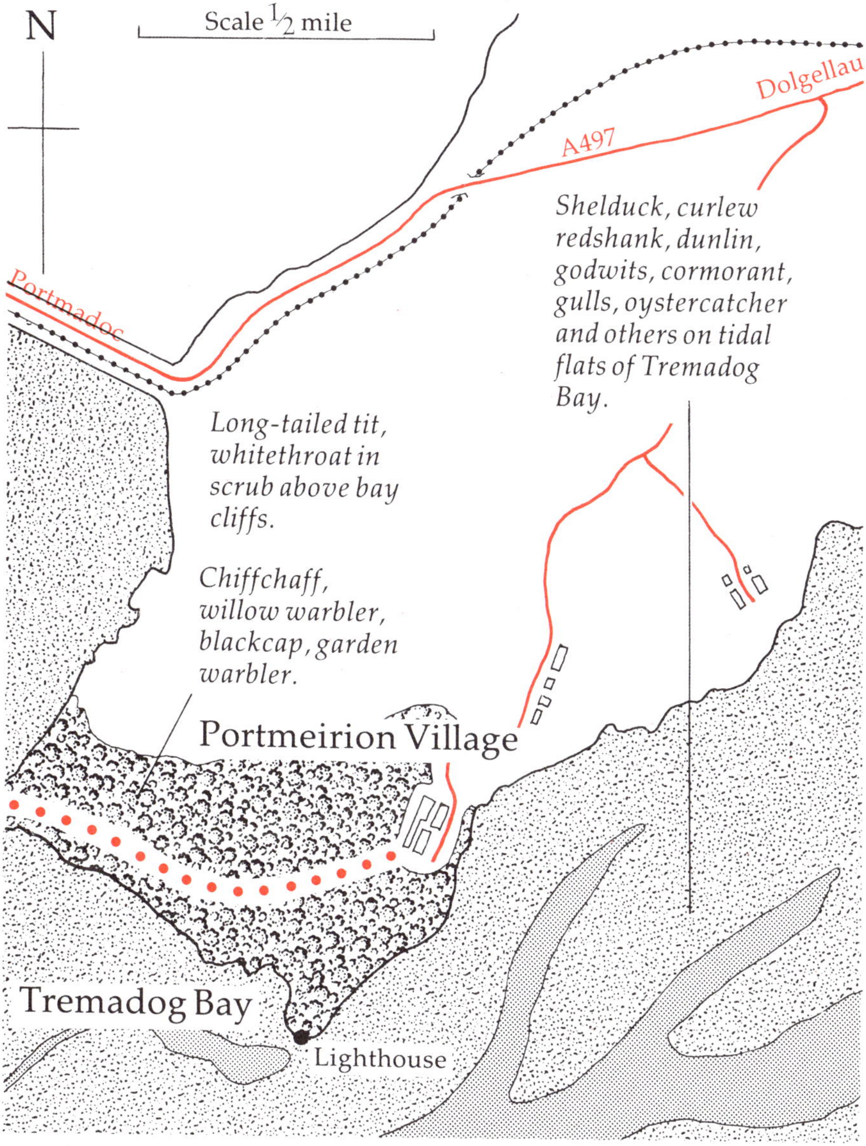

N

Scale ½ mile

Dolgellau

A497

Portmadoc

Shefduck, curlew redshank, dunlin, godwits, cormorant, gulls, oystercatcher and others on tidal flats of Tremadog Bay.

Long-tailed tit, whitethroat in scrub above bay cliffs.

Chiffchaff, willow warbler, blackcap, garden warbler.

Portmeirion Village

Tremadog Bay

Lighthouse

Take the marsh road across Morfa Harlech (A496) and find the small track from sharp bend in Llanfrangell y Traethau to the side of estuary. Car parking at end of track.

NNR

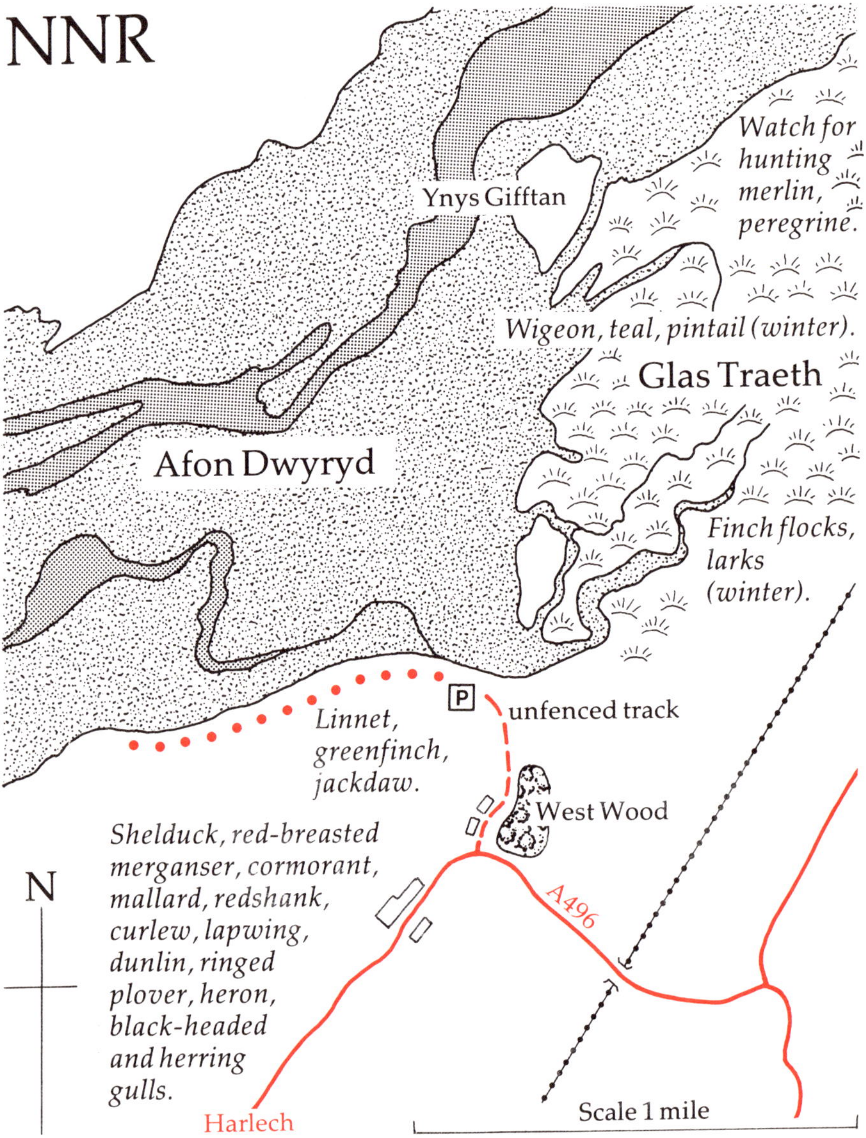

Watch for hunting merlin, peregrine.

Ynys Gifftan

Wigeon, teal, pintail (winter).

Glas Traeth

Afon Dwyryd

Finch flocks, larks (winter).

P   unfenced track

Linnet, greenfinch, jackdaw.

West Wood

Shelduck, red-breasted merganser, cormorant, mallard, redshank, curlew, lapwing, dunlin, ringed plover, heron, black-headed and herring gulls.

N

A496

Harlech

Scale 1 mile

On A496 between Ffestiniog and Blaenau Ffestiniog. Foothills of the Moelwyn Mts. A good birdwatching area and a beautiful walk.

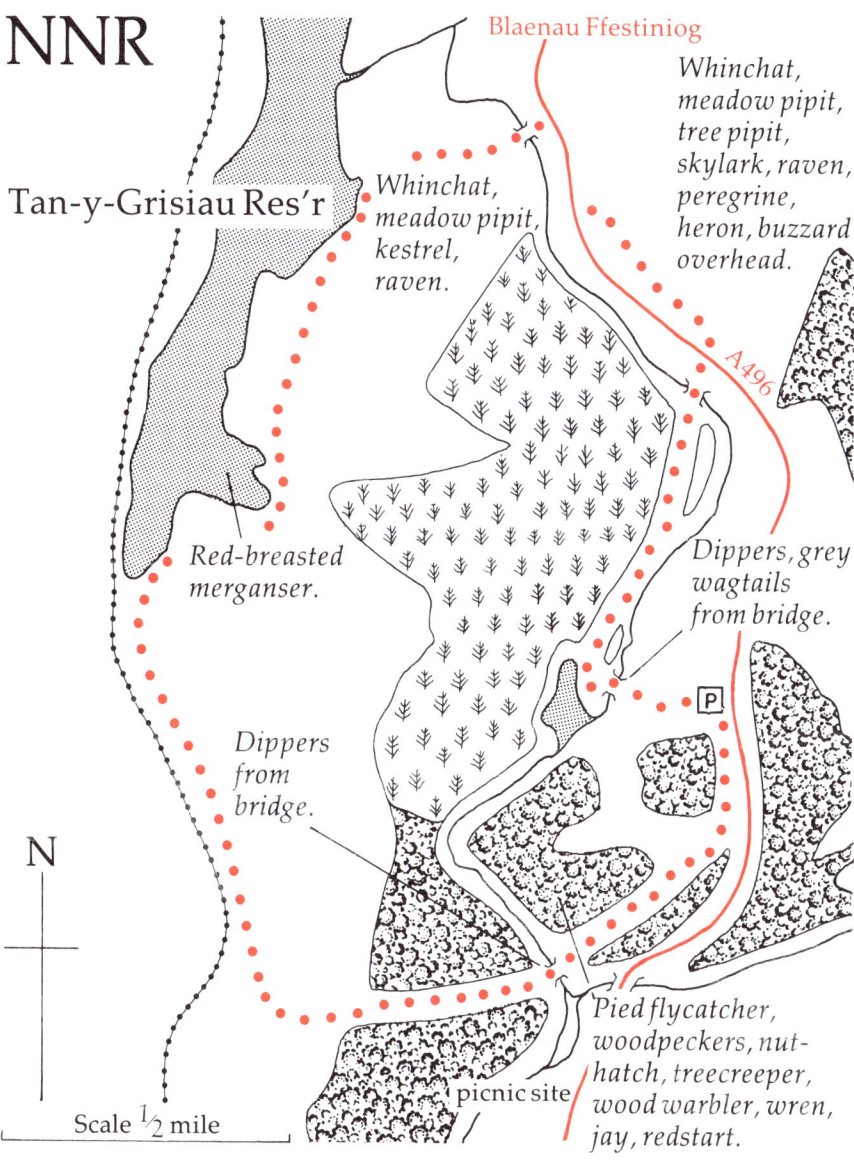

NNR

Tan-y-Grisiau Res'r

Blaenau Ffestiniog

Whinchat, meadow pipit, tree pipit, skylark, raven, peregrine, heron, buzzard overhead.

Whinchat, meadow pipit, kestrel, raven.

A496

Red-breasted merganser.

Dippers, grey wagtails from bridge.

Dippers from bridge.

P

N

Scale ½ mile

Pied flycatcher, woodpeckers, nuthatch, treecreeper, wood warbler, wren, jay, redstart.

picnic site

Plas Tan-y-Bwlch is the National park Centre near Maentwrog. Magnificent oak woodlands and river valley. Beautiful Llyn Mair is ½ mile along B4410 road towards Rhyd.

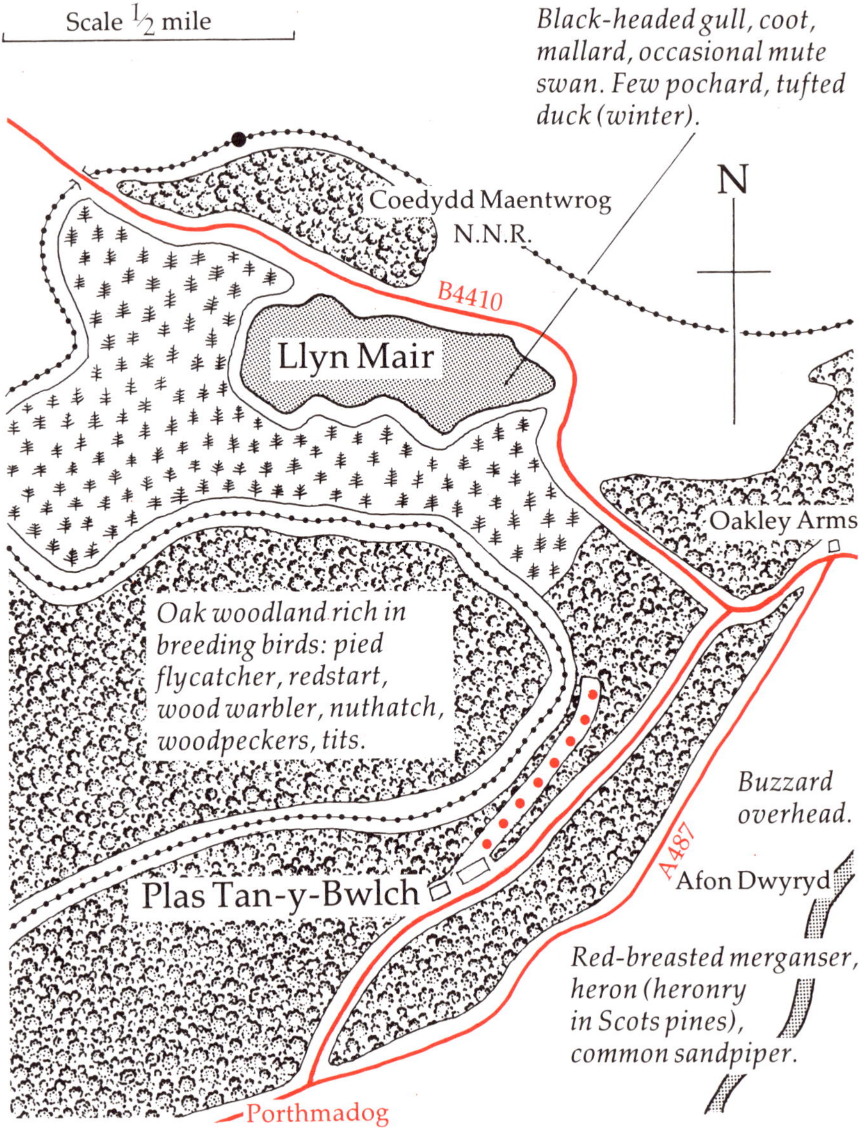

Scale ½ mile

Black-headed gull, coot, mallard, occasional mute swan. Few pochard, tufted duck (winter).

Coedydd Maentwrog N.N.R.

B4410

N

Llyn Mair

Oakley Arms

Oak woodland rich in breeding birds: pied flycatcher, redstart, wood warbler, nuthatch, woodpeckers, tits.

Buzzard overhead.

A487

Afon Dwyryd

Plas Tan-y-Bwlch

Red-breasted merganser, heron (heronry in Scots pines), common sandpiper.

Porthmadog

29

Best birdwatching from nature trail or dam and footbridge (S.end).
Nature trail leaflets at Power Station gatehouse.

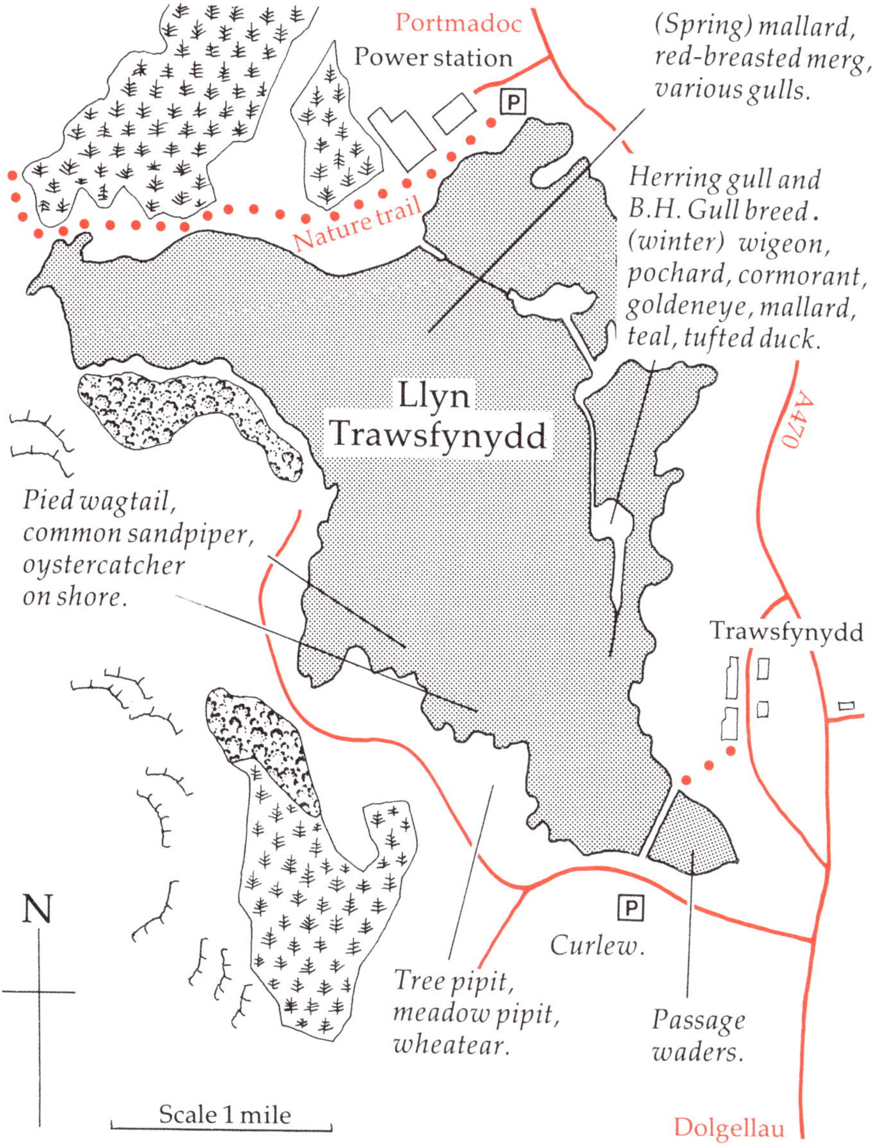

Portmadoc

Power station

P

*(Spring) mallard,
red-breasted merg,
various gulls.*

*Herring gull and
B.H. Gull breed.
(winter) wigeon,
pochard, cormorant,
goldeneye, mallard,
teal, tufted duck.*

Nature trail

Llyn
Trawsfynydd

A470

*Pied wagtail,
common sandpiper,
oystercatcher
on shore.*

Trawsfynydd

P

Curlew.

N

*Tree pipit,
meadow pipit,
wheatear.*

*Passage
waders.*

Scale 1 mile

Dolgellau

30

Access (no vehicles) along track from Llyn Cottage (limited parking) on B4470 Festiniog – Pentrefoelas Road at GR SH 782447. Llyn Conwy lies in the middle of extensive, desolate moorland. Do not leave the track in poor visibility.

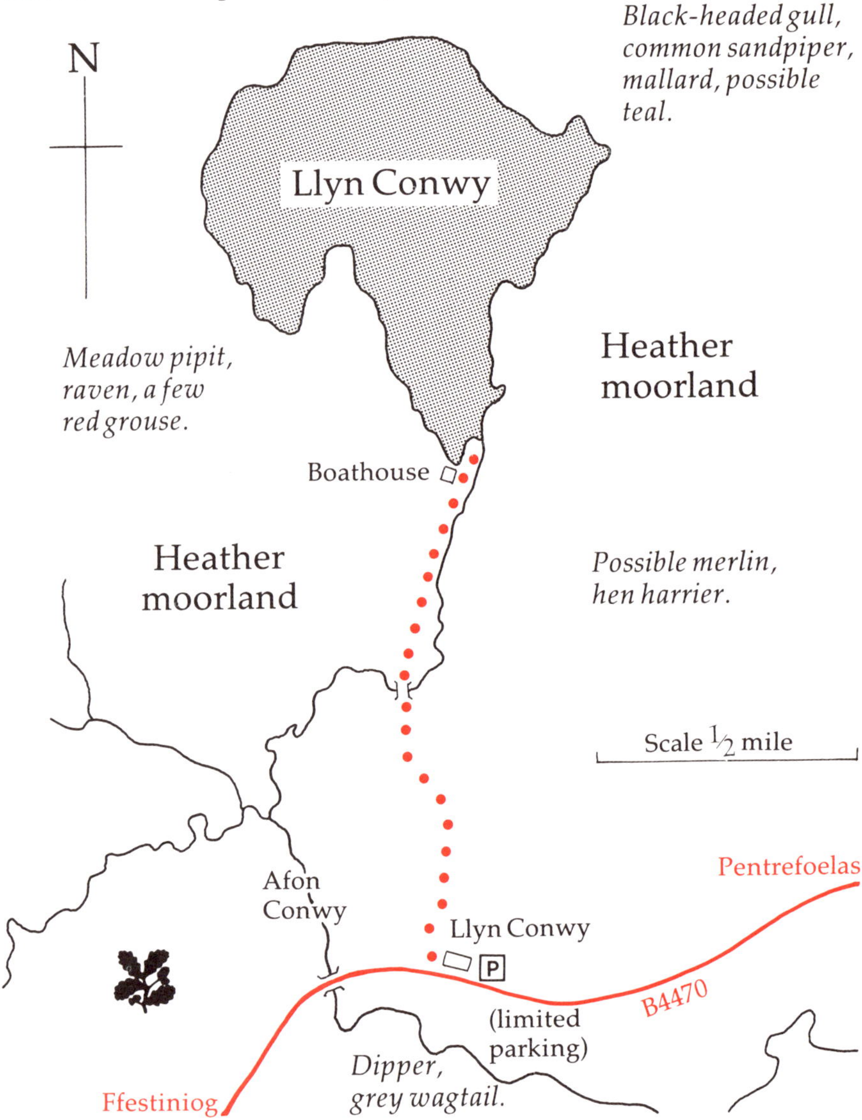

Black-headed gull, common sandpiper, mallard, possible teal.

N

Llyn Conwy

Meadow pipit, raven, a few red grouse.

Heather moorland

Boathouse

Heather moorland

Possible merlin, hen harrier.

Scale $^1/_2$ mile

Pentrefoelas

Afon Conwy

Llyn Conwy

P

(limited parking)

B4470

Ffestiniog

Dipper, grey wagtail.

31

Llyn Tegid (Bala Lake) is good for birds at either end (especially small bay at SW corner). B4391 on S.side (or the Bala Lake railway) give best views.

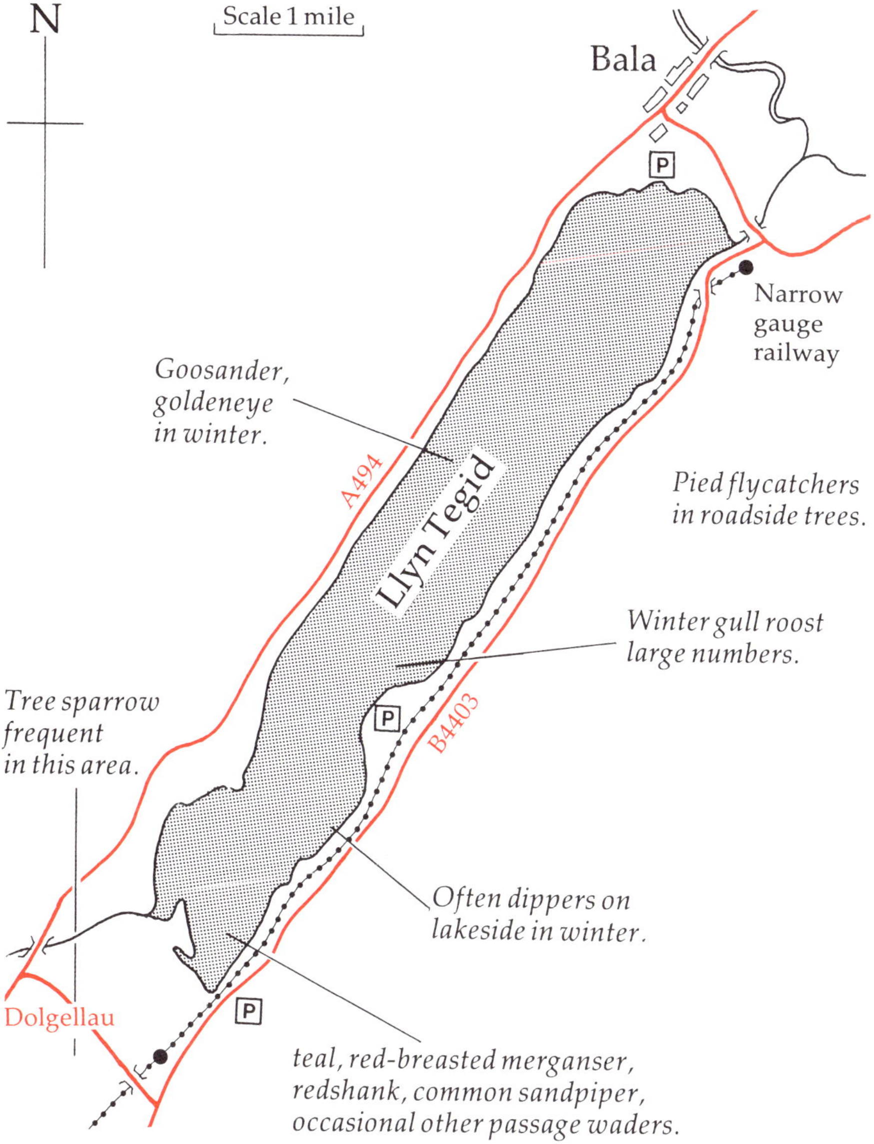

N

Scale 1 mile

Bala

P

Narrow gauge railway

Goosander, goldeneye in winter.

A494

Llyn Tegid

Pied flycatchers in roadside trees.

Winter gull roost large numbers.

Tree sparrow frequent in this area.

P

B4403

Often dippers on lakeside in winter.

Dolgellau

P

teal, red-breasted merganser, redshank, common sandpiper, occasional other passage waders.

MORFA HARLECH

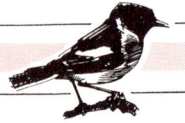

Access into Morfa Harlech national Nature Reserve is by the minor road next to the school on A496 below the town. Park at end of road.

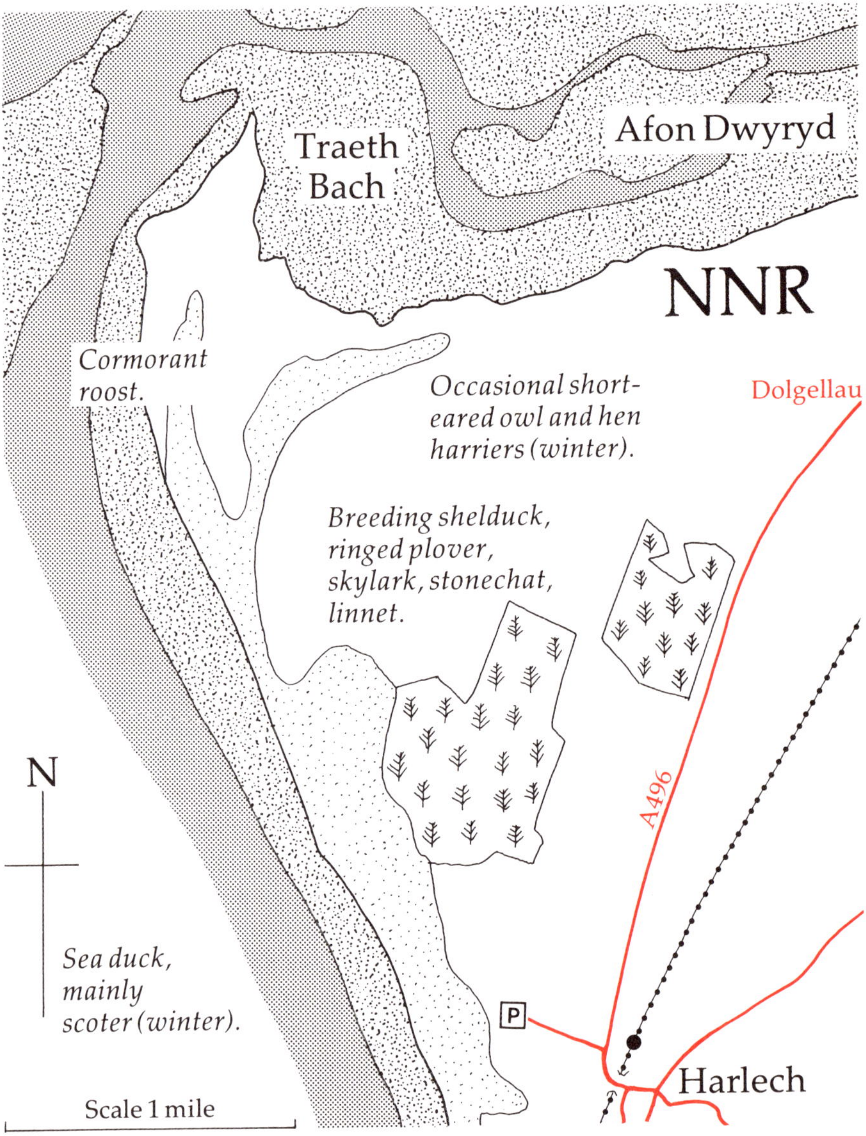

Traeth Bach
Afon Dwyryd
NNR
Cormorant roost.
Occasional short-eared owl and hen harriers (winter).
Dolgellau
Breeding shelduck, ringed plover, skylark, stonechat, linnet.
A496
N
Sea duck, mainly scoter (winter).
P
Harlech
Scale 1 mile

ROMAN STEPS

Take Cwm Bychan turning in Llanbedr village, 4 miles S. of Harlech. Follow 'Roman Steps' footpath from car park to top of pass, and return. Mountain walk but easy and rewarding.

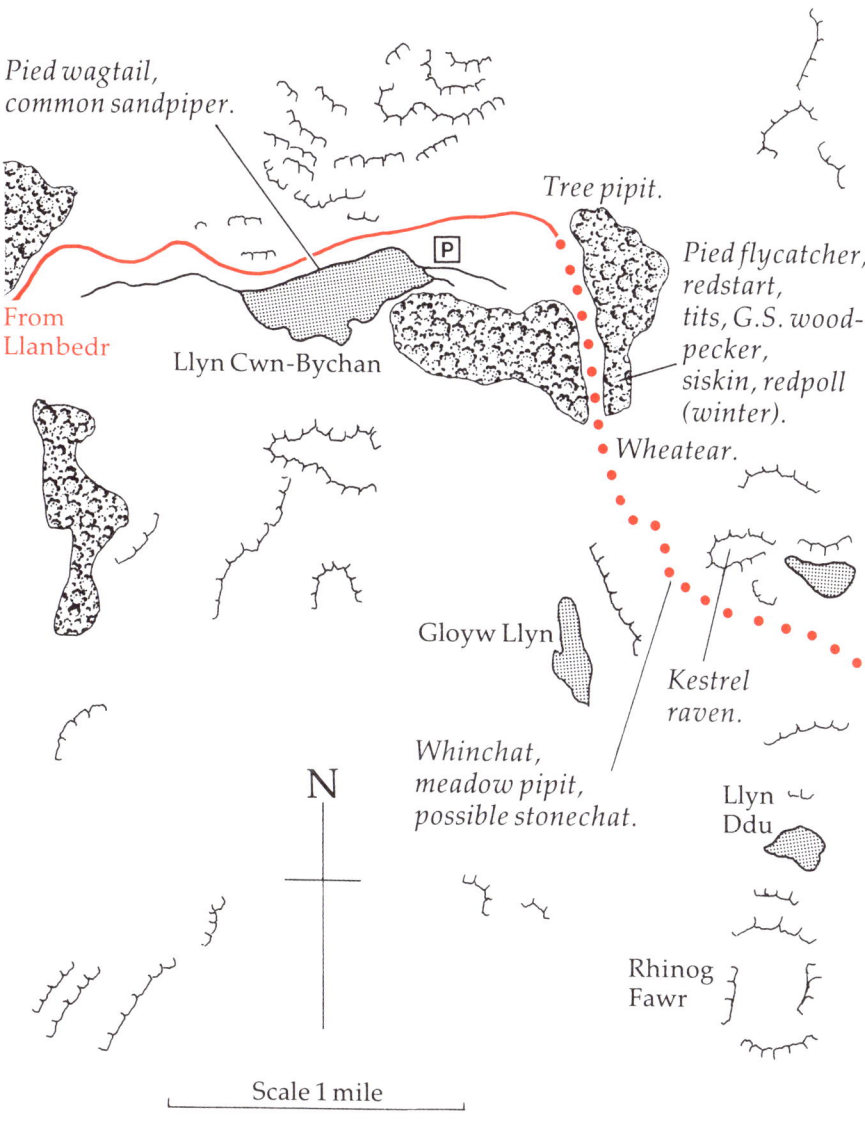

Pied wagtail, common sandpiper.

Tree pipit.

P

From Llanbedr

Llyn Cwn-Bychan

Pied flycatcher, redstart, tits, G.S. wood-pecker, siskin, redpoll (winter).

Wheatear.

Gloyw Llyn

Kestrel raven.

N

Whinchat, meadow pipit, possible stonechat.

Llyn Ddu

Rhinog Fawr

Scale 1 mile

DOLGEFEILIAU

Maesgwm Forest Centre and Dolgefeiliau Picnic site on A470 7 miles
N of Dolgellau. Excellent deer-watching hide (good for birds too) is
also available by prior arrangement.

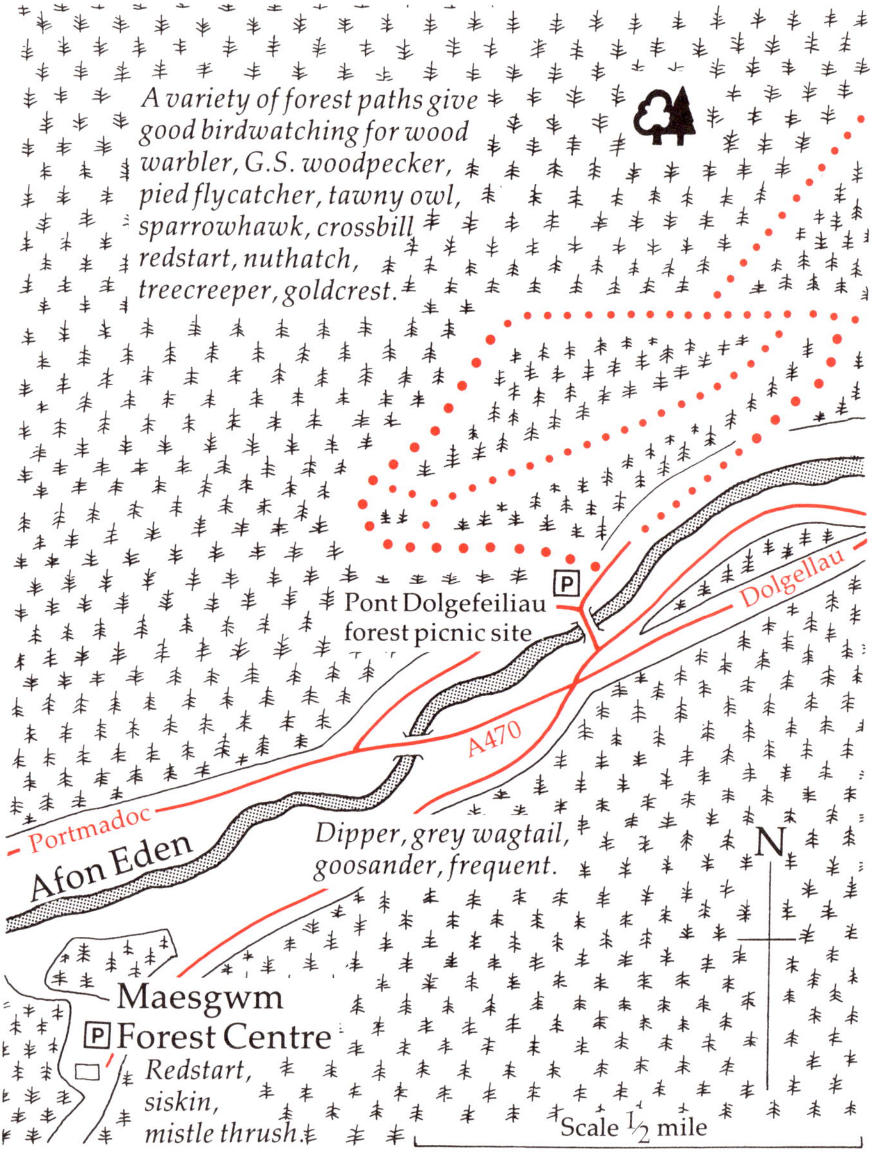

*A variety of forest paths give
good birdwatching for wood
warbler, G.S. woodpecker,
pied flycatcher, tawny owl,
sparrowhawk, crossbill
redstart, nuthatch,
treecreeper, goldcrest.*

P Pont Dolgefeiliau
forest picnic site

Dolgellau

A470

Portmadoc

Afon Eden

*Dipper, grey wagtail,
goosander, frequent.*

N

Maesgwm
P Forest Centre

*Redstart,
siskin,
mistle thrush.*

Scale $\frac{1}{2}$ mile

TY'N-Y-GROES

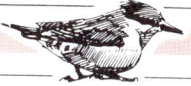

Turn off the A470 Dolgellau – Porthmadog road just N. of Ty'n-Y-Groes Hotel (6 miles N. Dolgellau) and cross Afon Mawddach. Fine forest walks and varied birds.

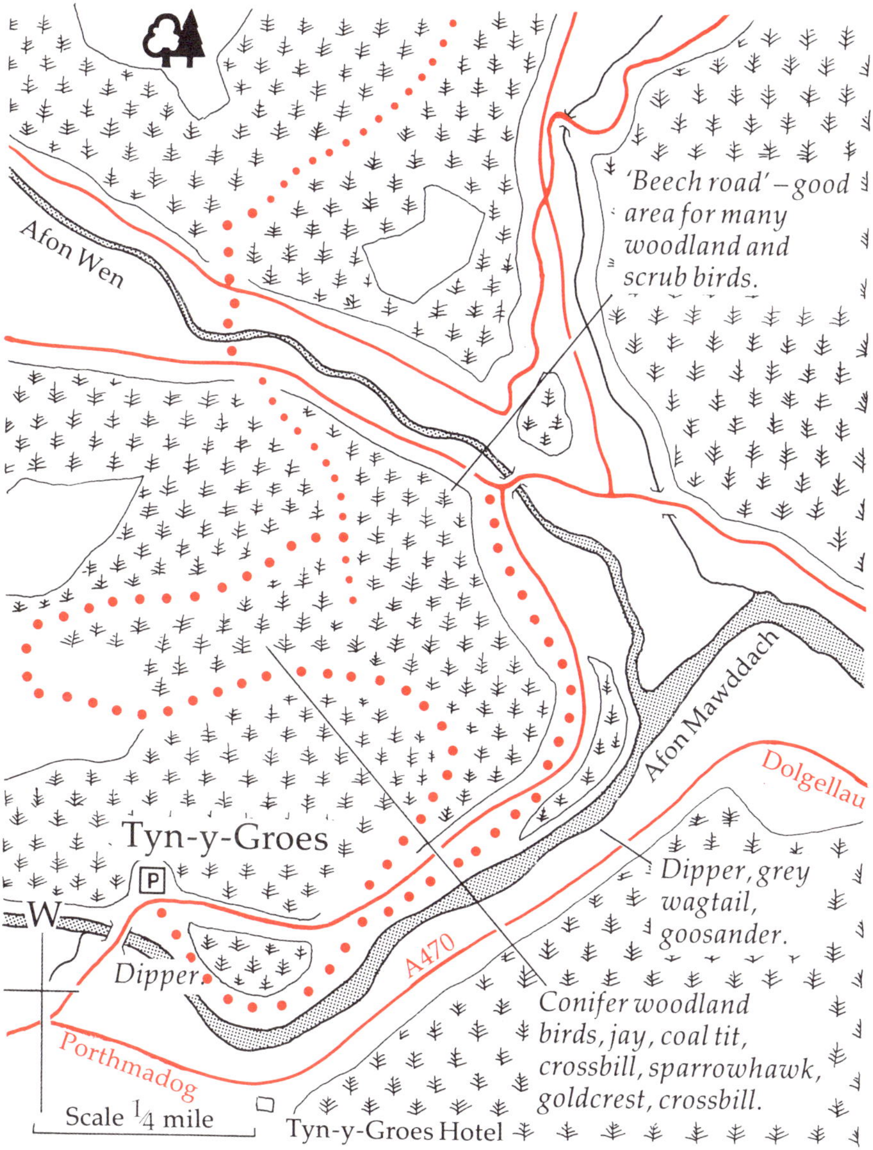

Afon Wen
'Beech road' – good area for many woodland and scrub birds.
Tyn-y-Groes
P
W
Dipper.
Afon Mawddach
Dolgellau
Dipper, grey wagtail, goosander.
A470
Conifer woodland birds, jay, coal tit, crossbill, sparrowhawk, goldcrest, crossbill.
Porthmadog
Scale 1/4 mile
Tyn-y-Groes Hotel

DOLMELYNLLYN

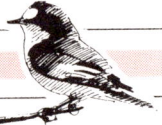

Dolmelynllyn is a National Trust property at Ganllwyd on A470 6 miles N. of Dolgellau. Many paths through fine oak woods and torrent streams. Open hill above.

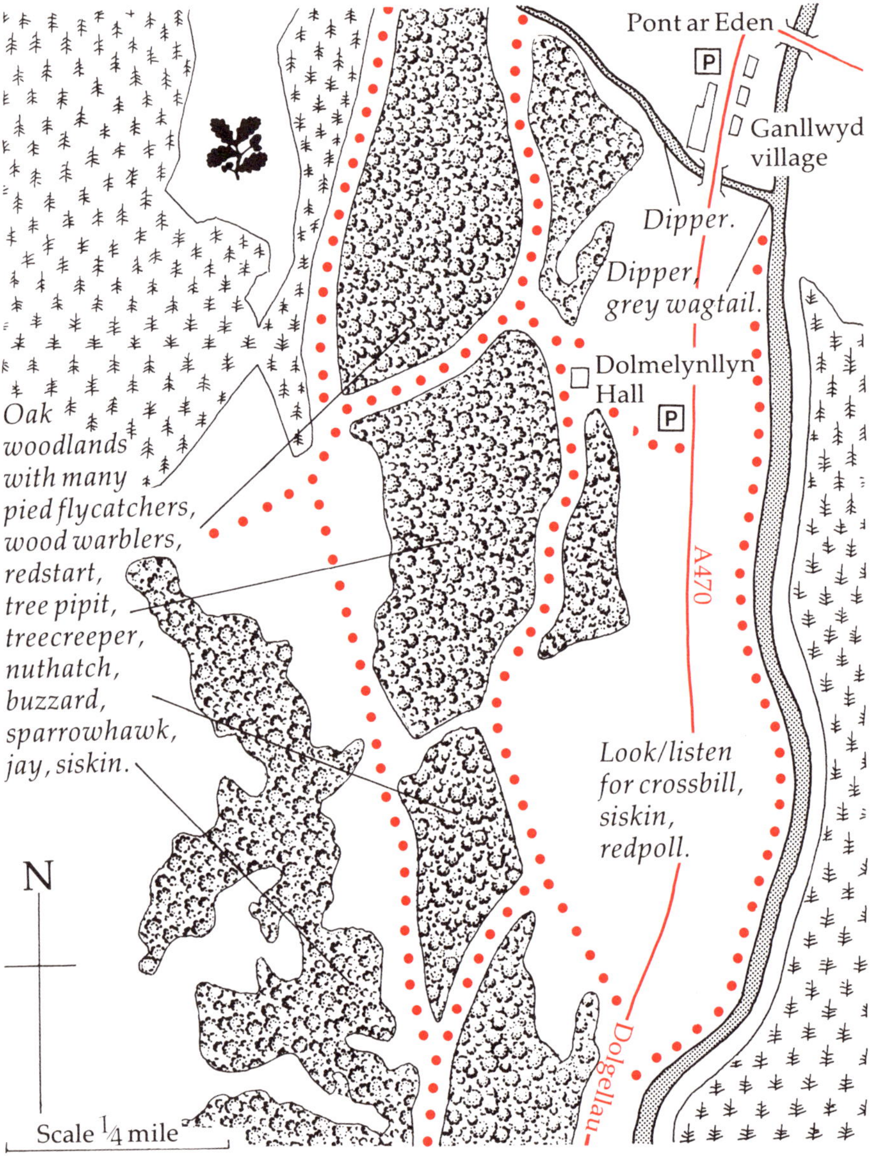

Pont ar Eden
P
Ganllwyd village
Dipper.
Dipper, grey wagtail.
Dolmelynllyn Hall
P
A470
Oak woodlands with many pied flycatchers, wood warblers, redstart, tree pipit, treecreeper, nuthatch, buzzard, sparrowhawk, jay, siskin.
Look/listen for crossbill, siskin, redpoll.
N
Scale 1/4 mile
Dolgellau

MAWDDACH VALLEY

This map shows the location of the four sites in the Mawddach valley which are featured on the following pages.

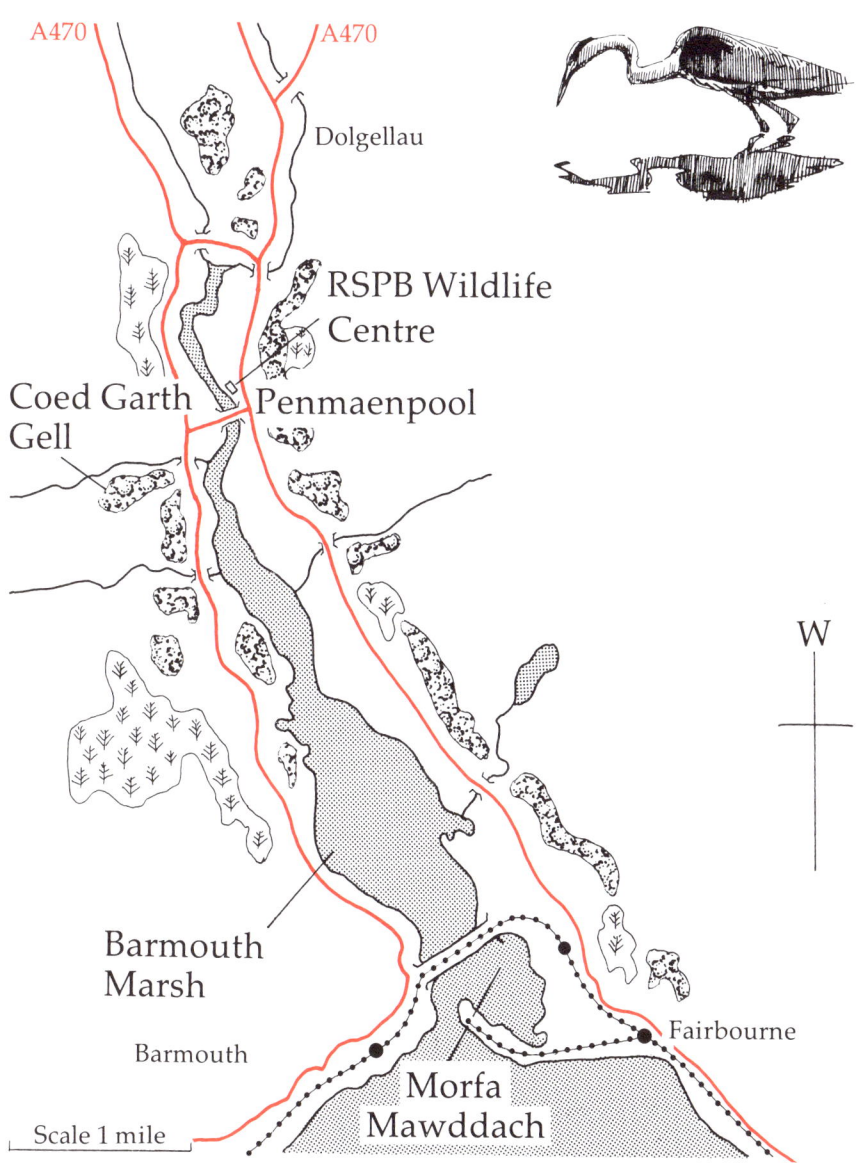

A470

A470

Dolgellau

RSPB Wildlife
Centre

Coed Garth
Gell

Penmaenpool

W

Barmouth
Marsh

Barmouth

Fairbourne

Morfa
Mawddach

Scale 1 mile

COED GARTH GELL

The entrance to this RSPB reserve is adjacent to the lay-by on A496
Dolgellau – Barmouth road, opposite Borthwnog Hall Hotel, 4 miles
west of Dolgellau. Park in lay-by.

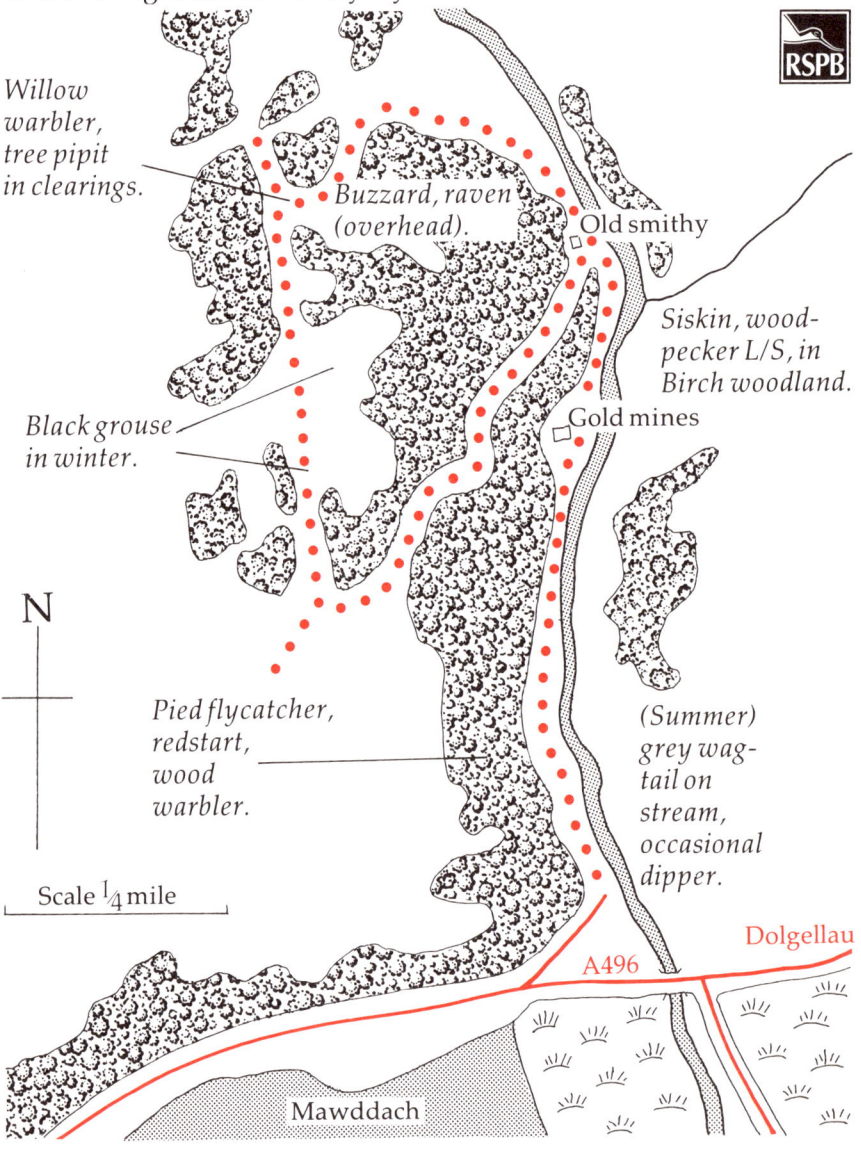

*Willow
warbler,
tree pipit
in clearings.*

*Buzzard, raven
(overhead).*

Old smithy

RSPB

*Siskin, wood-
pecker L/S, in
Birch woodland.*

*Black grouse
in winter.*

Gold mines

N

*Pied flycatcher,
redstart,
wood
warbler.*

*(Summer)
grey wag-
tail on
stream,
occasional
dipper.*

Scale ¼ mile

Dolgellau

A496

Mawddach

MORFA MAWDDACH

View Morfa Mawddach from car park at end of road through Fairbourne village. Good views of waders etc. from here. Also good sea watching spot.

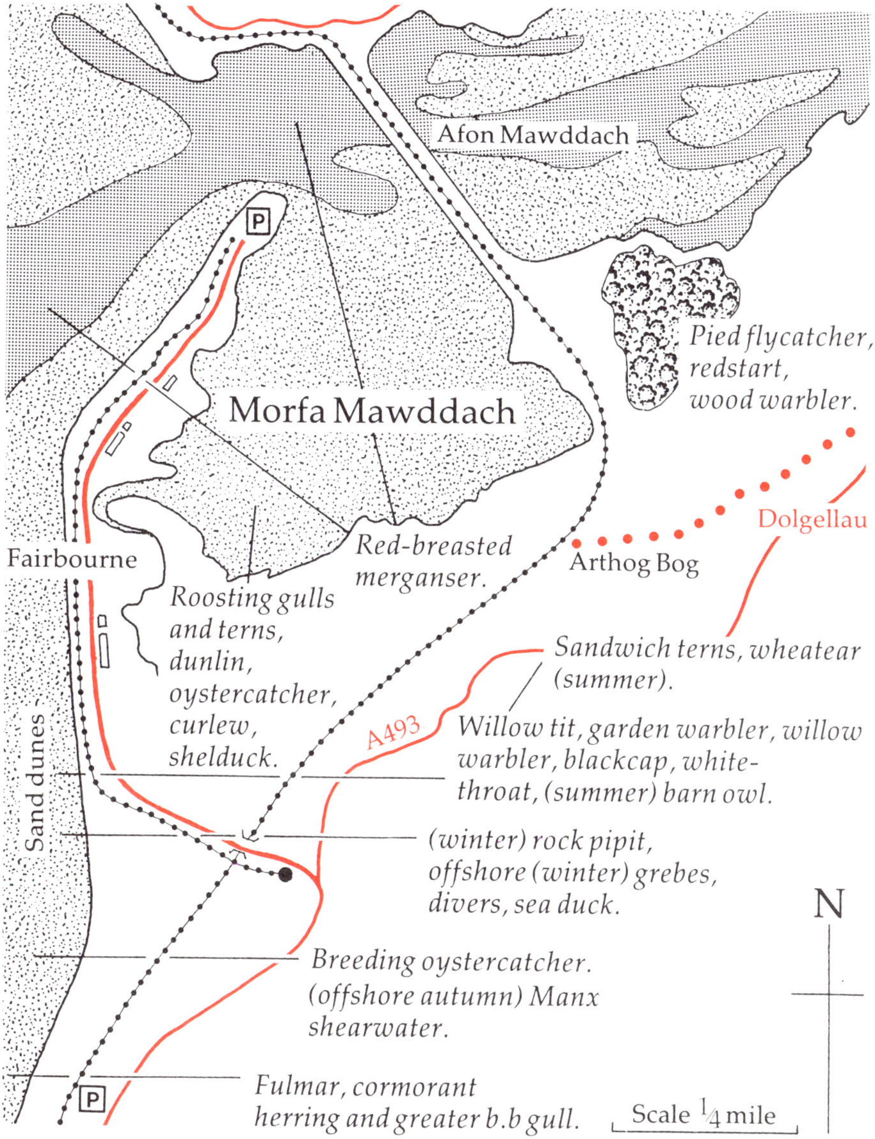

Afon Mawddach

P

Pied flycatcher, redstart, wood warbler.

Morfa Mawddach

Dolgellau

Fairbourne

Red-breasted merganser.

Arthog Bog

Roosting gulls and terns, dunlin, oystercatcher, curlew, shelduck.

Sandwich terns, wheatear (summer).

Sand dunes

A493

Willow tit, garden warbler, willow warbler, blackcap, white-throat, (summer) barn owl.

(winter) rock pipit, offshore (winter) grebes, divers, sea duck.

N

Breeding oystercatcher. (offshore autumn) Manx shearwater.

P

Fulmar, cormorant herring and greater b.b gull.

Scale ¼ mile

Penmaenpool and the RSPB Wildlife Centre are on A493, 3 miles
west of Dolgellau.

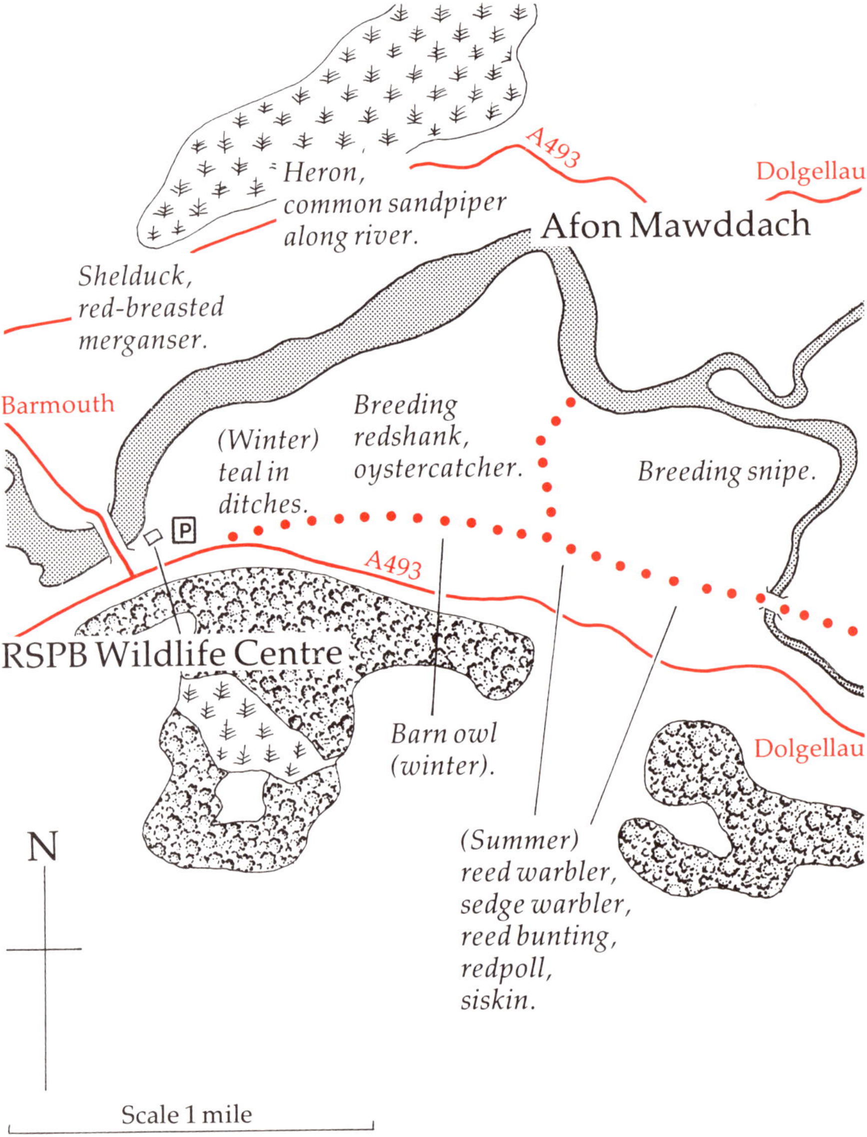

*Heron,
common sandpiper
along river.*

A493

Dolgellau

Afon Mawddach

*Shelduck,
red-breasted
merganser.*

Barmouth

*Breeding
redshank,
oystercatcher.*

*(Winter)
teal in
ditches.*

Breeding snipe.

A493

RSPB Wildlife Centre

*Barn owl
(winter).*

Dolgellau

*(Summer)
reed warbler,
sedge warbler,
reed bunting,
redpoll,
siskin.*

N

Scale 1 mile

Barmouth Marsh (or Cutiau Marsh) is on the Mawddach estuary alongside A496 2 miles E. of Barmouth. Park in lay-bys.

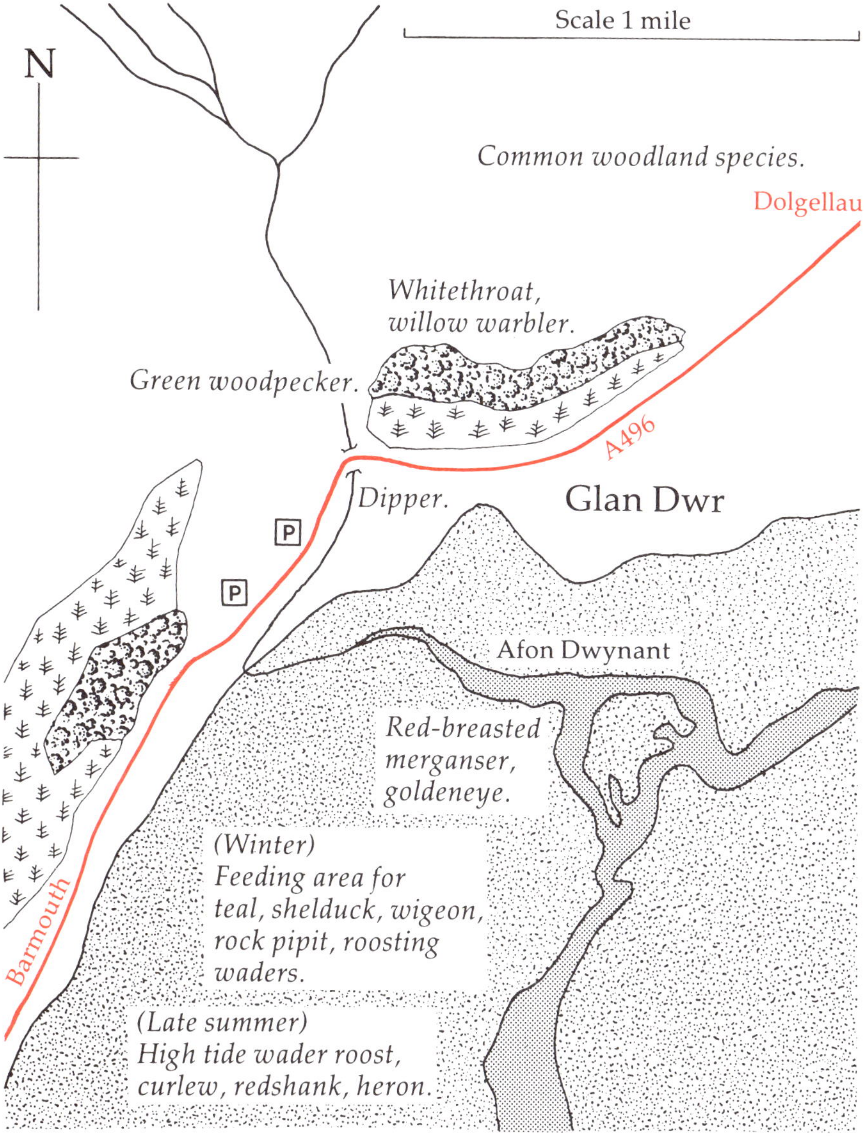

N

Scale 1 mile

Common woodland species.

Dolgellau

*Whitethroat,
willow warbler.*

Green woodpecker.

A496

Dipper.

Glan Dwr

P

P

Afon Dwynant

*Red-breasted
merganser,
goldeneye.*

*(Winter)
Feeding area for
teal, shelduck, wigeon,
rock pipit, roosting
waders.*

*(Late summer)
High tide wader roost,
curlew, redshank, heron.*

Barmouth

TORRENT WALK

The famous Torrent Walk is on Afon Clywedog by the hamlet of
Brithdir on B4416, 3 miles from Dolgellau on the Welshpool road.
Spectacular river section with oak woods and many birds.

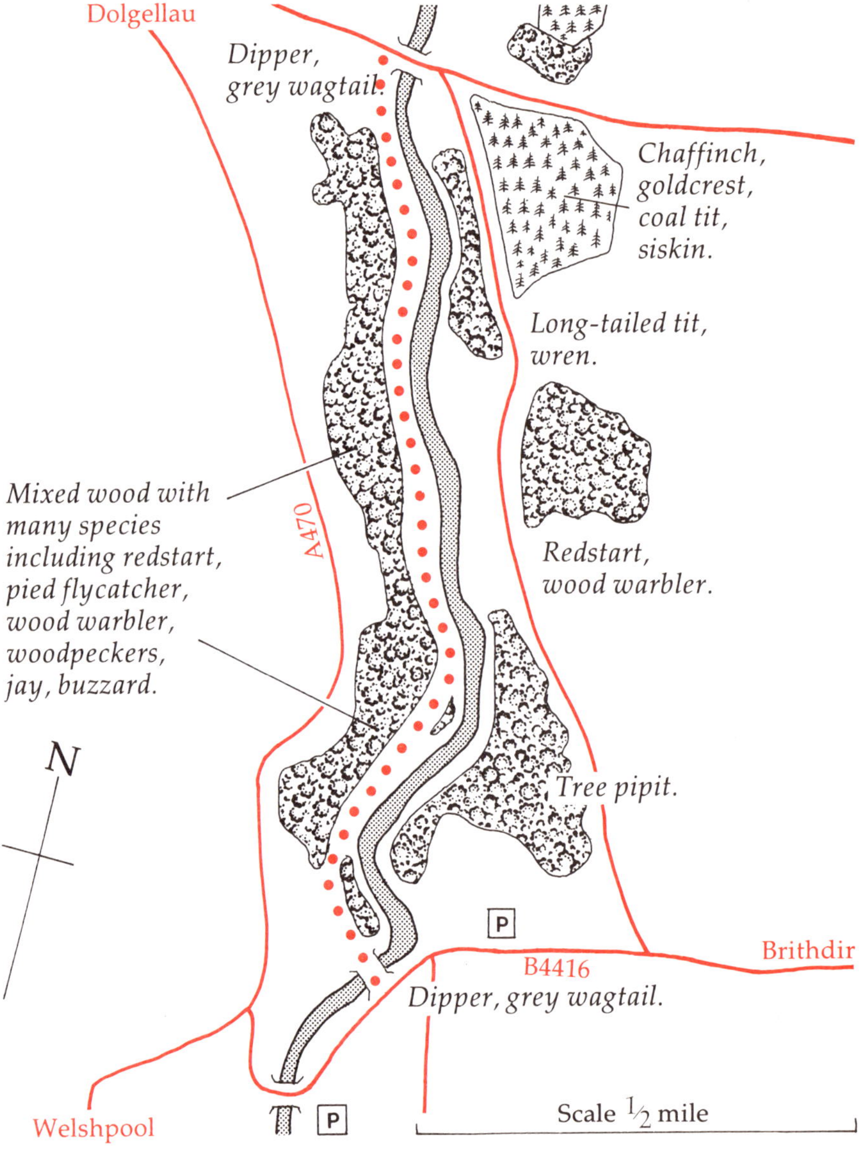

Dolgellau

*Dipper,
grey wagtail.*

*Chaffinch,
goldcrest,
coal tit,
siskin.*

*Long-tailed tit,
wren.*

A470

*Mixed wood with
many species
including redstart,
pied flycatcher,
wood warbler,
woodpeckers,
jay, buzzard.*

*Redstart,
wood warbler.*

N

Tree pipit.

P

Brithdir

B4416

Dipper, grey wagtail.

Welshpool

P

Scale $\frac{1}{2}$ mile

The Afon Dysynni flows to the sea just N. of Tywyn, passing through the strange tidal lake – The Broadwater.
Aberdysynni and Broadwater together are one of the best bird-watching places in the Park.

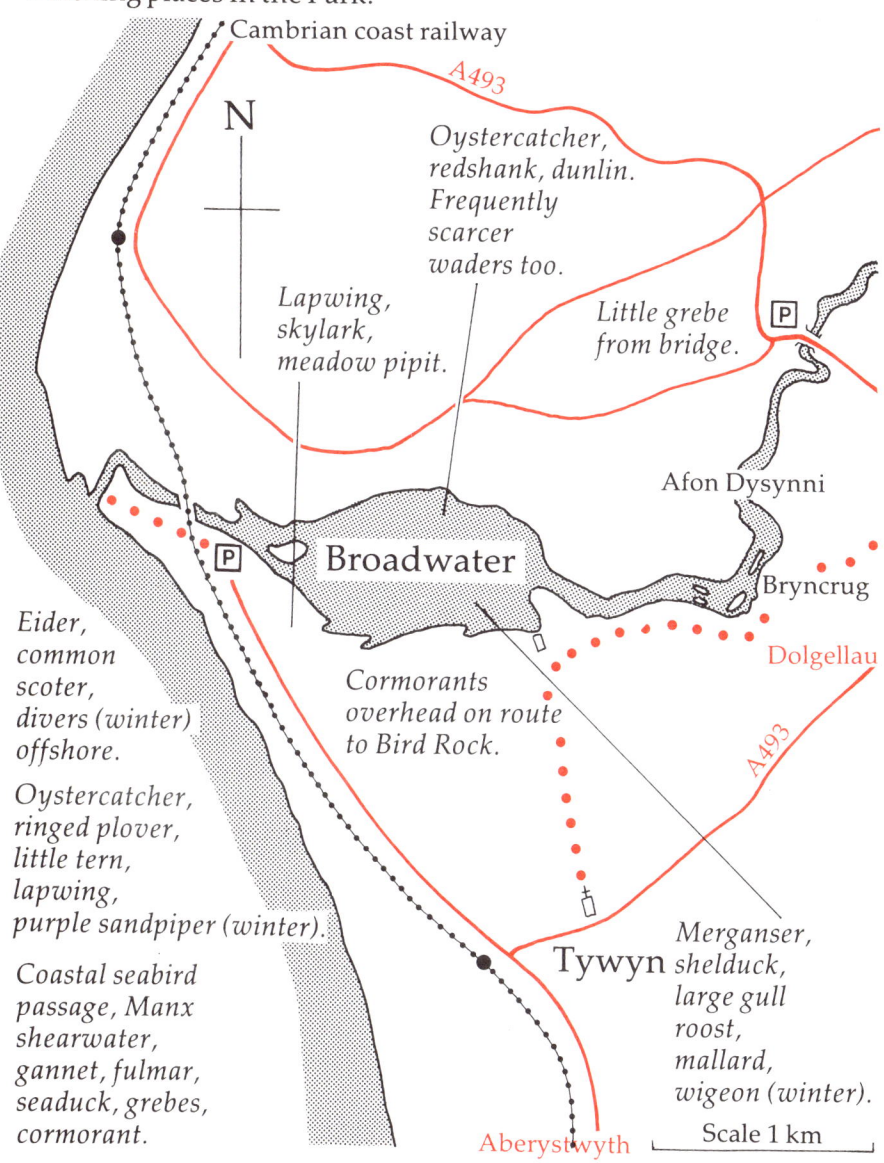

Cambrian coast railway

A493

N

Oystercatcher, redshank, dunlin. Frequently scarcer waders too.

Lapwing, skylark, meadow pipit.

Little grebe from bridge.

P

Afon Dysynni

P

Broadwater

Bryncrug

Eider, common scoter, divers (winter) offshore.

Cormorants overhead on route to Bird Rock.

Dolgellau

A493

Oystercatcher, ringed plover, little tern, lapwing, purple sandpiper (winter).

Coastal seabird passage, Manx shearwater, gannet, fulmar, seaduck, grebes, cormorant.

Tywyn

Merganser, shelduck, large gull roost, mallard, wigeon (winter).

Aberystwyth

Scale 1 km

Craig-yr-Aderyn (Bird Rock) is an impressive rugged landmark in the Dysynni valley inland from Tywyn. Good viewing achieved from roadside, with limited parking.

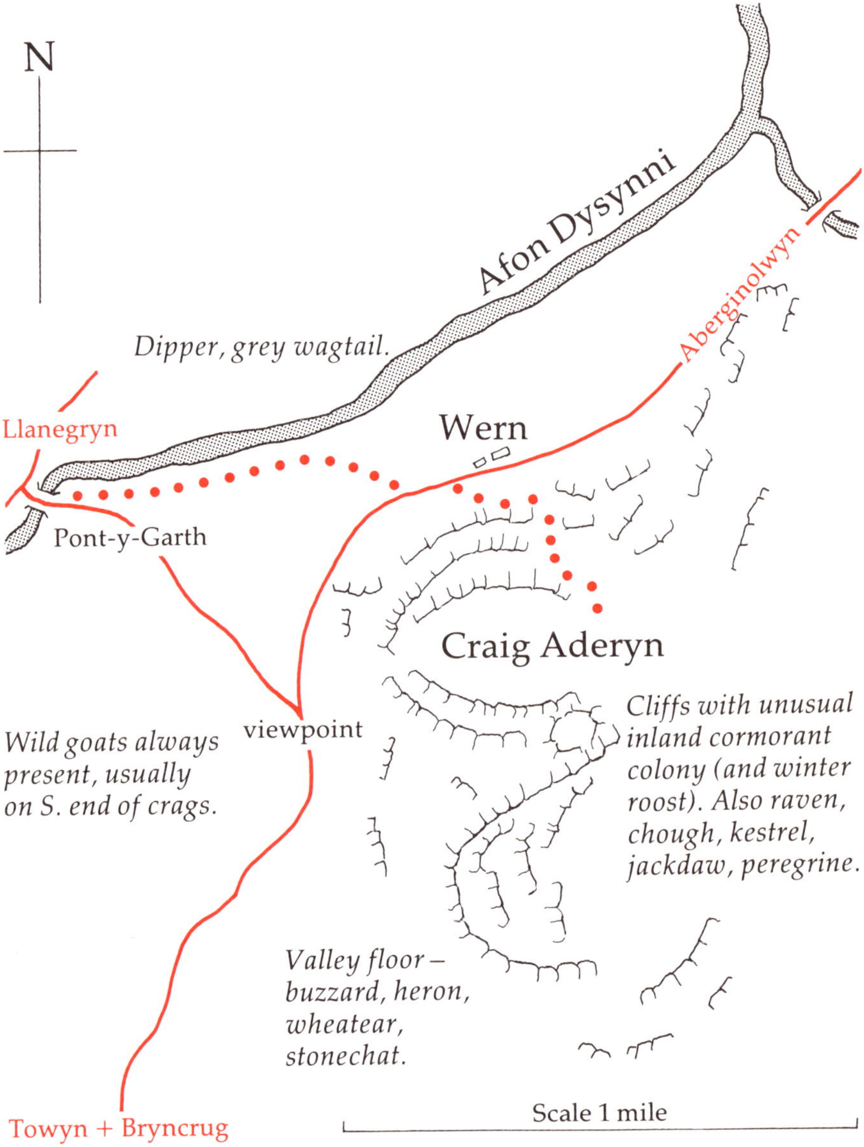

N

Afon Dysynni

Aberginolwyn

Dipper, grey wagtail.

Llanegryn

Wern

Pont-y-Garth

Craig Aderyn

Wild goats always present, usually on S. end of crags.

viewpoint

Cliffs with unusual inland cormorant colony (and winter roost). Also raven, chough, kestrel, jackdaw, peregrine.

Valley floor – buzzard, heron, wheatear, stonechat.

Scale 1 mile

Towyn + Bryncrug

44

LLYN MYNGWL

Llyn Myngwl (Tal-y-Llyn Lake) has good wildfowl at the top end
(furthest from hotel). Particularly notable for tufted duck, coot (up to
300) and pochard in winter.

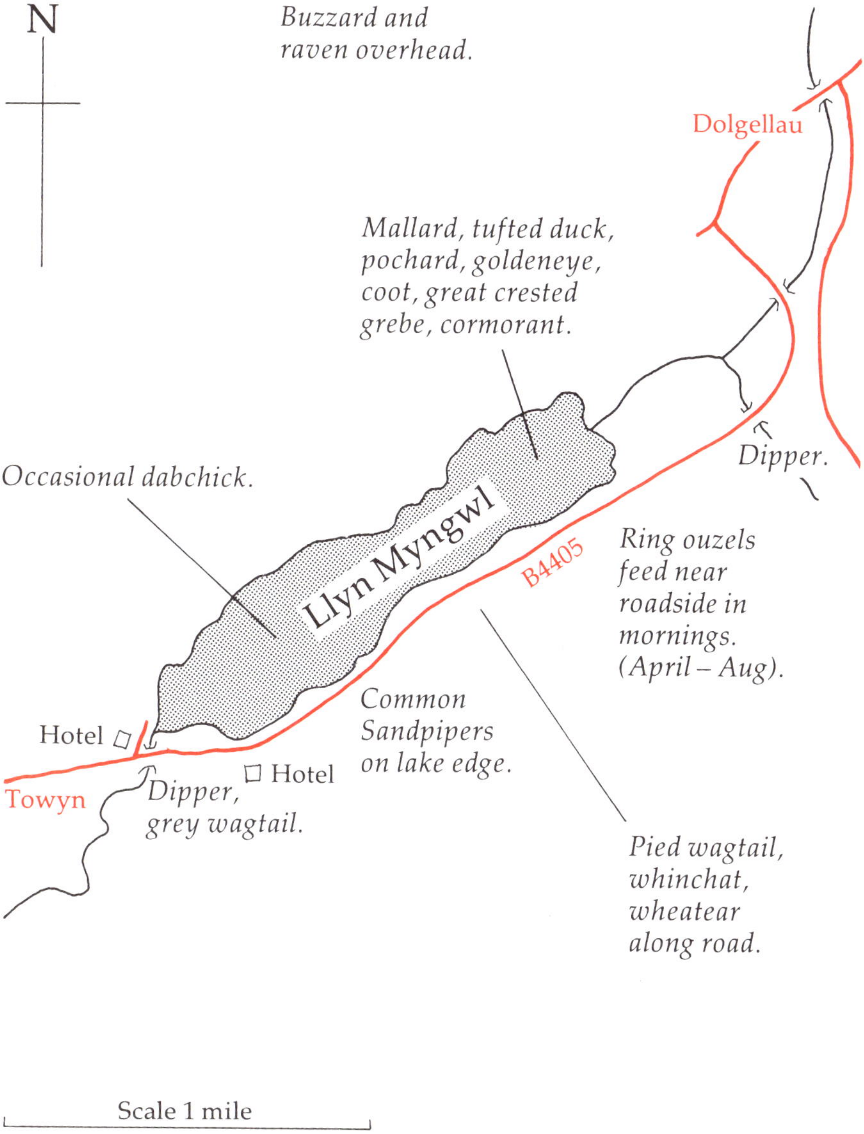

N

*Buzzard and
raven overhead.*

Dolgellau

*Mallard, tufted duck,
pochard, goldeneye,
coot, great crested
grebe, cormorant.*

Occasional dabchick.

Dipper.

Llyn Myngwl

B4405

*Ring ouzels
feed near
roadside in
mornings.
(April – Aug).*

*Common
Sandpipers
on lake edge.*

Hotel

Hotel

Towyn

*Dipper,
grey wagtail.*

*Pied wagtail,
whinchat,
wheatear
along road.*

Scale 1 mile

NANT GWERNOL

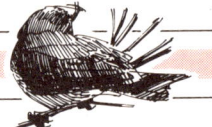

Nant Gwernol is the final stop on the Tal-y-Llyn Railway line. Signposted trails run into the forest from the station – either down the valley to Abergynolwyn or up to old quarries at Bryn Eglwys.

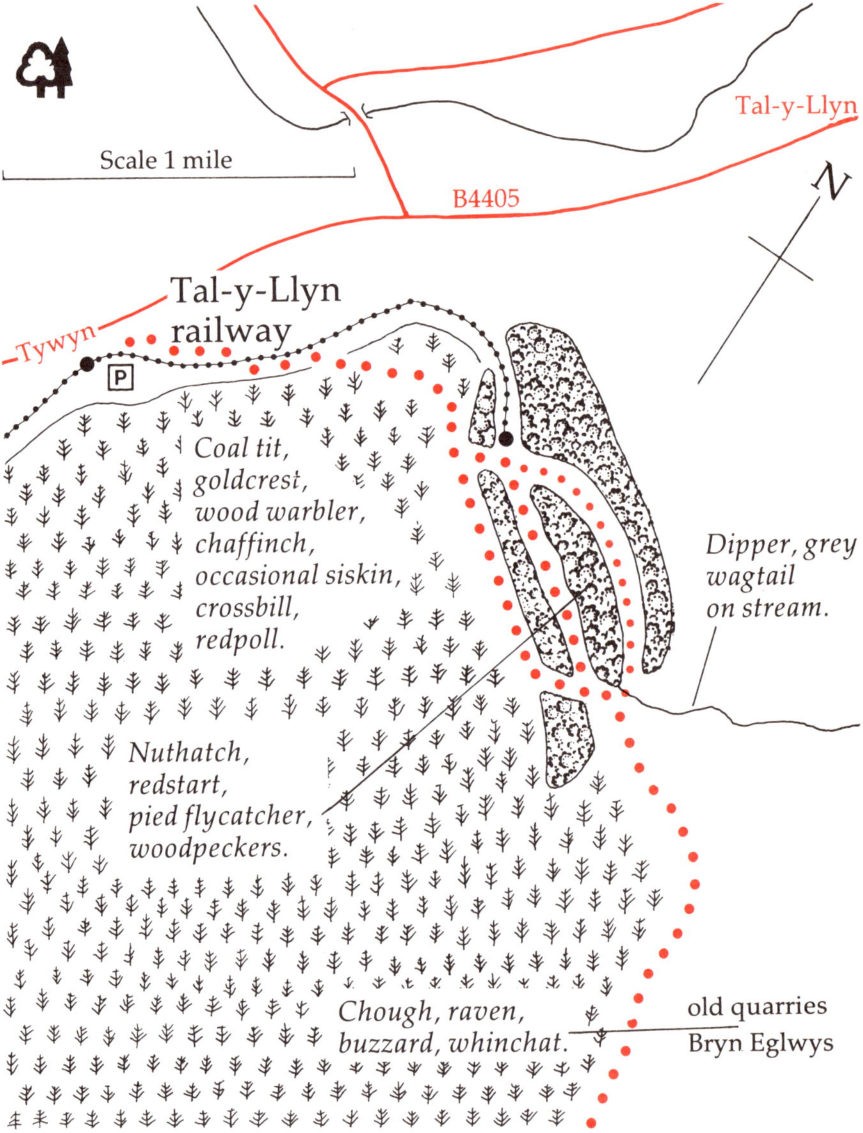

Scale 1 mile
Tal-y-Llyn
B4405
N
Tal-y-Llyn railway
Tywyn
P
Coal tit, goldcrest, wood warbler, chaffinch, occasional siskin, crossbill, redpoll.
Dipper, grey wagtail on stream.
Nuthatch, redstart, pied flycatcher, woodpeckers.
Chough, raven, buzzard, whinchat.
old quarries Bryn Eglwys

LAKE VYRNWY

Lake Vyrnwy RSPB Reserve, 16,000 acres moorland, woodlands and open water. Visitor centre open daily in spring and summer. Many paths and trails. Outstanding area for birds.

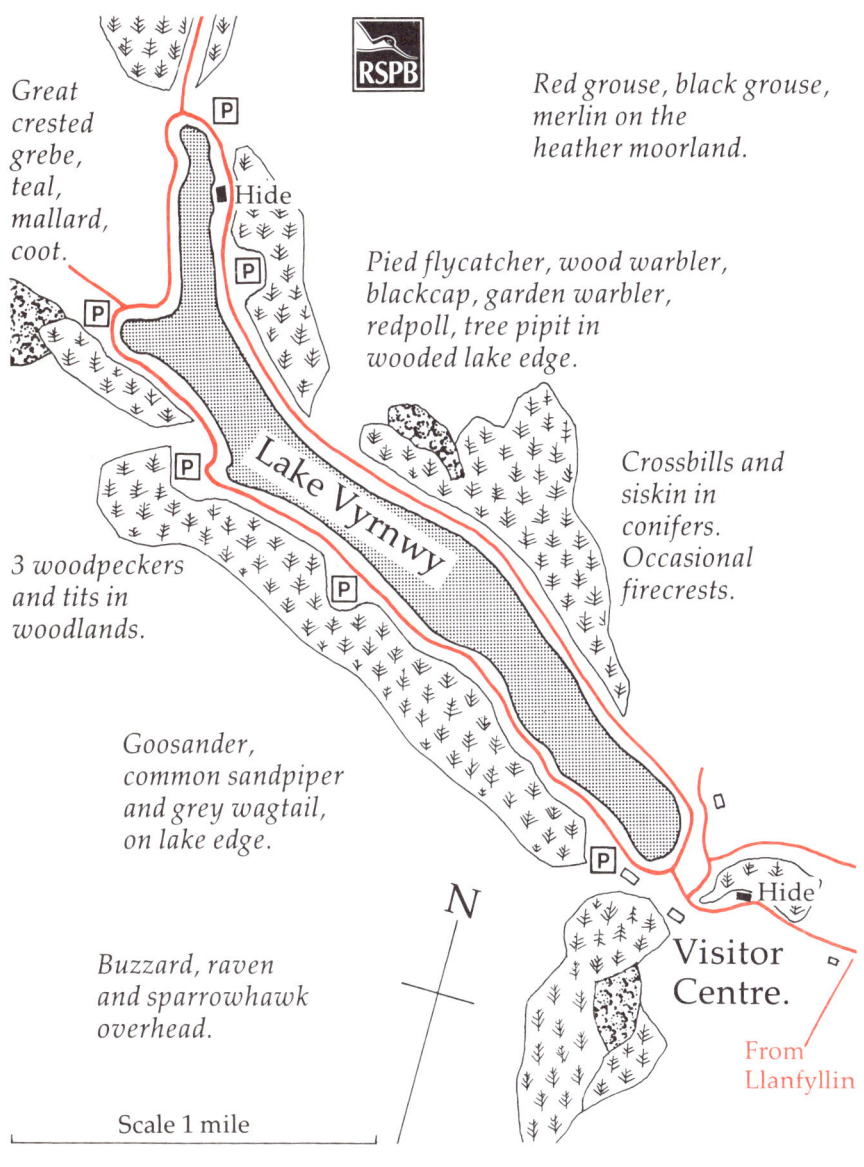

Great crested grebe, teal, mallard, coot.

RSPB

Red grouse, black grouse, merlin on the heather moorland.

Hide

Pied flycatcher, wood warbler, blackcap, garden warbler, redpoll, tree pipit in wooded lake edge.

Lake Vyrnwy

Crossbills and siskin in conifers. Occasional firecrests.

3 woodpeckers and tits in woodlands.

Goosander, common sandpiper and grey wagtail, on lake edge.

N

Buzzard, raven and sparrowhawk overhead.

Hide

Visitor Centre.

From Llanfyllin

Scale 1 mile

47

CWM CADIAN

The Tan-y-Coed (Forestry Commission) picnic site 3 miles N. of Machynlleth on A487 Dolgellau road gives access to the splendid Cwm Cadian area of Dyfi Forest.

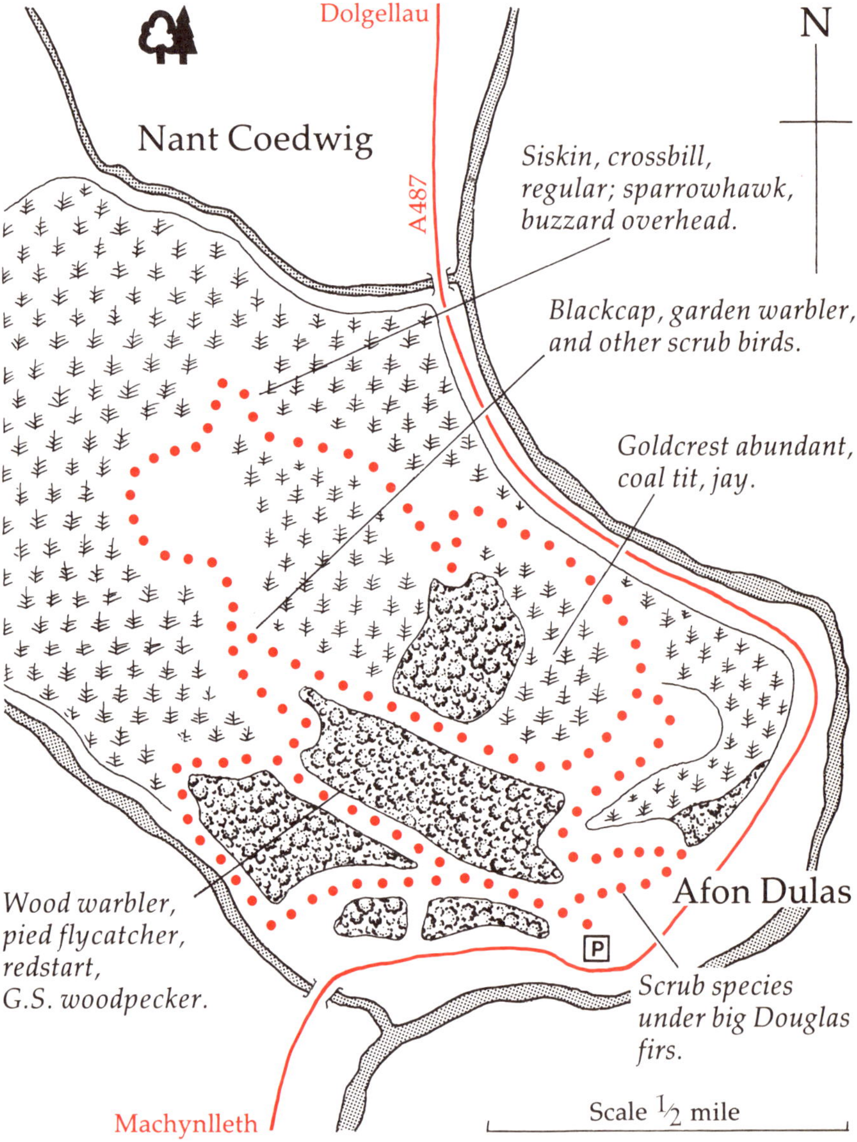

Dolgellau

N

Nant Coedwig

A487

Siskin, crossbill, regular; sparrowhawk, buzzard overhead.

Blackcap, garden warbler, and other scrub birds.

Goldcrest abundant, coal tit, jay.

Afon Dulas

Wood warbler, pied flycatcher, redstart, G.S. woodpecker.

P

Scrub species under big Douglas firs.

Machynlleth

Scale $^1/_2$ mile

YNYS-HIR

Ynys Hir RSPB reserve is signposted in the hamlet of Eglwysfach, 8 miles S. of Machynlleth. First rate for birds all year.

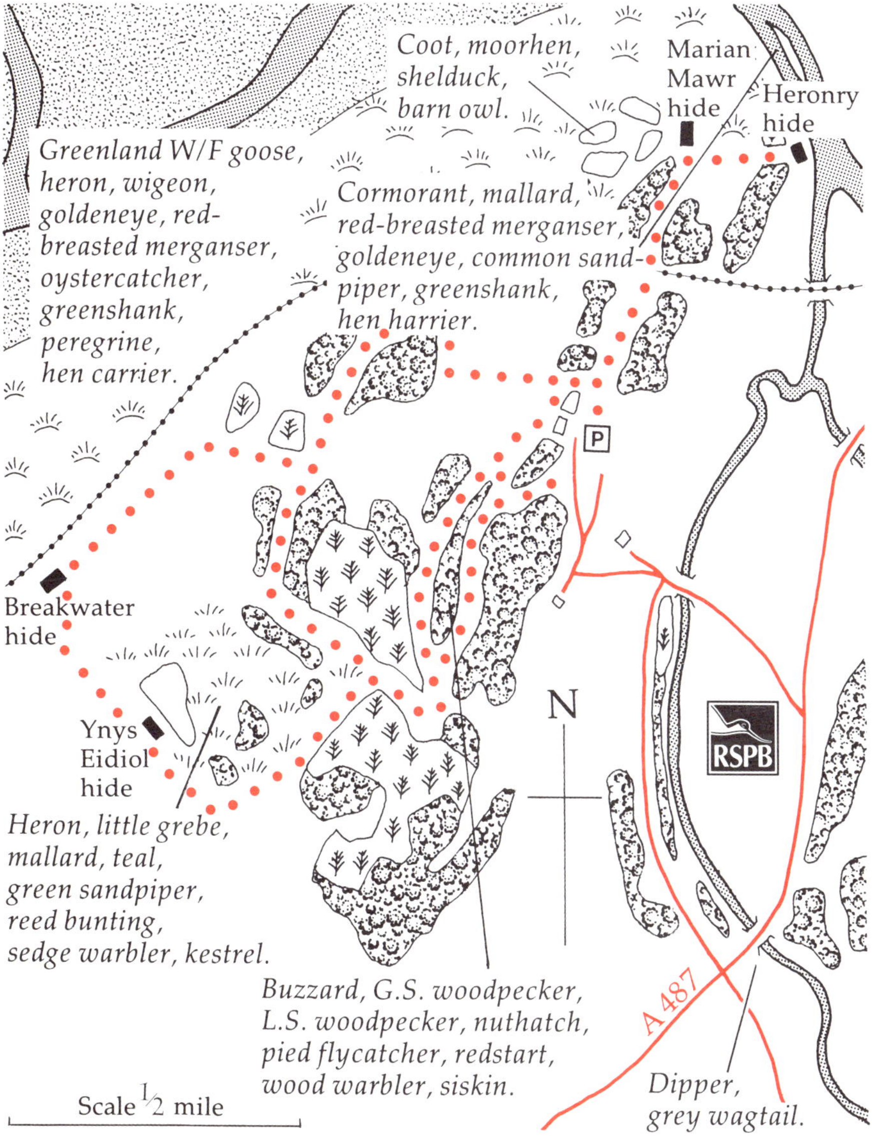

Coot, moorhen, shelduck, barn owl.

Marian Mawr hide

Heronry hide

Greenland W/F goose, heron, wigeon, goldeneye, red-breasted merganser, oystercatcher, greenshank, peregrine, hen carrier.

Cormorant, mallard, red-breasted merganser, goldeneye, common sand-piper, greenshank, hen harrier.

P

Breakwater hide

Ynys Eidiol hide

Heron, little grebe, mallard, teal, green sandpiper, reed bunting, sedge warbler, kestrel.

N

RSPB

Buzzard, G.S. woodpecker, L.S. woodpecker, nuthatch, pied flycatcher, redstart, wood warbler, siskin.

A 487

Dipper, grey wagtail.

Scale ¹⁄₂ mile

49

Several important RSPB reserves and information centres are open to the public in North Wales and Mid Wales (RSPB members enter free to most). All are exciting places to see birds most of the year. Three RSPB reserves are featured in this book, namely Coed Garth Gell (map 38), Lake Vyrnwy (map 47) and Ynys-hir (map 49). Others which lie outside the Snowdonia region are listed below.

Dyffryn Wood (SN 980672) and **Corngafallt Common** (SN 9464), Rhayader, Powys. Access at all times. Dyffryn Wood is on the side of the A470 and Corngafallt Common is accessible along public footpaths from minor roads between Llanwrthwl and Elan Village.

Point of Air, Clwyd Viewpoint for birdwatching at end of Station Road off A548 at Talacre SJ 113833. Extensive views over the outer part of the Dee estuary which is one of the most important estuary sites for birds in western Britain.

dotterel

goldcrest and firecrest

Gayton Sands, Clwyd (SJ 274789) Take B5135 to Parkgate off A540 Chester-Hoylake road and then turn right at Boathouse Restaurant. Good views over the Dee Marshes from the Old Baths car park and the adjacent public footpath.

South Stack Cliffs, Gwynedd Access at all times. Roads signposted from Holyhead SH 205823. Seabird colonies and fine heathland. Choughs and peregrines are regular.

Ellin's Tower Information Centre, South Stack. This spectacular cliff-edge information centre overlooks the seabird colonies. Open daily from 11 am to 5 pm, April-September.

'Wild Snowdonia' ('Eryri Wyllt') RSPB information and interpretation centre in the National Park Information Centre at Betws-y-Coed. Open daily (admission 50p adult, 25p child). Film, audio-visual, children's room, large bank of data on wildlife in the Snowdonia National Park.

BIRDWATCHERS' CODE OF CONDUCT

Today's birdwatchers are a powerful force for nature conservation. The number of those of us interested in birds rises continually and it is vital that we take seriously our responsibility to avoid any harm to birds.

We must also present a responsible image to non-birdwatchers who may be affected by our activities and particularly those on whose sympathy and support the future of birds rests.

There are 10 points to bear in mind:

1. The welfare of birds must come first.
2. Habitat must be protected.
3. Keep disturbance to birds and their habitat to a minimum.
4. When you find a rare bird think carefully about whom you should tell.
5. Do not harrass rare migrants.
6. Abide by the bird protection laws at all times.
7. Respect the rights of landowners.
8. Respect the rights of other people in the country-side.
9. Make your records available to the local bird recorder.
10. Behave abroad as you would when birdwatching at home.

The Young Ornithologists' Club

'Join the YOC and help protect birds — you'll have a great time too!'

Full of fun, the YOC is a club that will show you the world of birds in a new, fresh way. You will see birds you have never seen before — and learn fascinating new things about the ones you know well.

The YOC will give you:

Your own smart magazine. The award-winning *Bird Life* is the special magazine for YOC members and it's brilliant! Full of colour photographs, fascinating facts and wildlife tips from the experts it will be posted directly to you six times a year.

Bumper Bird Pack. Join now and you will get your first bonus copy of *Bird Life* FREE, a wallchart, a booklet full of fascinating tips, your official membership card and armbadge plus much more — all this inside our new 'Barn Owl' presentation wallet.

Good friends. Many YOC members get together in groups or at school and have a good time. You'll have the chance to visit exciting places all over Britain as well as joining the fun and activities near to home. Films, birdwatching trips, weekend activities, holiday courses and fun evenings: just some of the things that give everyone the chance to make new friends and meet wildlife experts.

Prizes and projects. You can enter competitions, or any one of dozens of quizzes with super prizes on offer. The YOC organises important work too. You can help us to discover more about birds and the problems they face.

And there's lots more for you to discover! You will be part of Europe's largest bird protection society. The YOC is the junior section of the Royal Society for the Protection of Birds. The RSPB is non-profit making and fights to protect all our wild birds, both here and abroad, from the many dangers they face. Birds and other wildlife need our help and care to survive in the modern world.

YOU CAN HELP BY JOINING THE YOC TODAY

More details overleaf...

Yes! I would like to join in the fun and activities of the YOC

First names   Date of Birth

_____   _____

_____   _____

_____   _____

_____   _____

_____   _____

Family surname _____

Address _____

_____

_____ Postcode _____

*Please find enclosed £4 (YOC Individual for anyone under 16
years)
£5 (YOC Family for any number of
brothers and sisters at one address)

* Delete as appropriate

I/we look forward to receiving a Bumper Bird Pack and official
YOC membership card and armbadge(s).

Payable to RSPB.

**RSPB/YOC, The Lodge,
Sandy, Beds, SG19 2DL**   658   **RSPB**

IMPORTANT FACTS ABOUT THE RSPB

The Royal Society for the Protection of Birds is Europe's largest voluntary wildlife conservation body. It is a registered charity, governed by an elected Council and supported by a subscribing membership of over half a million.

- It was founded in 1889 and incorporated under Royal Charter in 1904.

- It owns or leases over 120 reserves, covering more than 142,000 acres, most of which are open to members free of charge.

- It informs people about birds through films, publications, exhibitions and talks.

- It runs the Young Ornithologists' Club for young people of 16 and under.

- It undertakes research into the many problems facing wild birds today.

- It publicises and helps to enforce the bird protection laws.

- It investigates environmental effects on birds, advising government and industry.

- It co-operates with national and international conservation organisations both in the UK and abroad.

- It has a national network of local representatives and members' groups in most parts of the UK.

- It has a national network of regional offices throughout the UK.

- It sells a fine range of gifts, many of exclusive design, and all the profits go straight towards bird protection.

You can help by joining us in our fight for a better world for birds and people. In return you will:

- receive our popular, colour magazine, *Birds,* free four times a year

- have free admission to most of our reserves

- find an absorbing interest for you and your family

- be eligible to join the countryside network of lively members' groups and attend the annual members' conference and regional meetings

- receive details of the wide range of gifts marketed by our sales department, both mail order and through our shops

- be helping to protect wild birds for future generations to enjoy!

Join the RSPB today by completing the application form overleaf.

Free home extensions.

A Bedroom

A Bathroom

Choose one of these superb gifts, and it's yours with our compliments when you join the RSPB through this advertisement.

For £12 annual membership you will also receive our glossy magazine *Birds*, four times a year. Plus free entry to over 70 RSPB nature reserves.

And most importantly, you will be helping protect Britain's countryside and the birds that live there.

So whether you want to help raise a family or have a bath in your back garden, send off your application today.

I wish to join the RSPB and enclose my 1st year's subscription of £12. I select the following item as my free gift. (Special pensioner rates available, but excluding free gifts.) ☐ Nestbox ☐ Bird Bath

I would simply like to buy the following item(s)

☐ Nestbox (£5.95 inc. p&p) ☐ Bird Bath (£5.70 inc p&p)

Please allow 28 days for delivery. I enclose cheque/PO (payable to RSPB) or debit my Access/Visa Card No.⎯⎯⎯⎯⎯⎯⎯

(Please quote address of cardholder if different from below)

for a total of £ ⎯⎯⎯⎯⎯⎯

Cardholder's signature ⎯⎯⎯⎯⎯⎯⎯⎯⎯⎯⎯⎯⎯⎯

Name ⎯⎯⎯⎯⎯⎯⎯⎯⎯⎯⎯⎯⎯⎯

Block Capitals Please

Address ⎯⎯⎯⎯⎯⎯⎯⎯⎯⎯⎯⎯

⎯⎯⎯⎯⎯⎯⎯⎯ Postcode ⎯⎯⎯⎯⎯

658

Send to Royal Society for the Protection of Birds, Freepost, The Lodge, Sandy, Beds. SG19 2BR. Reg. Charity 207076

RSPB